What others are saying about this book:

"Your Performing Edge has all of the ingredients for self - psychological fine tuning. JoAnn Dahlkoetter has compiled her research into an easy application program for athletes of all levels. This isn't just a fluffy overview of psychological theories. *Your Performing Edge* is the ultimate book for attaining optimal mind-body performance. It's a great addition for myself and the athletes I teach."
Dave Scott, Six-time winner, Hawaii Ironman Triathlon

"A positive mental attitude is critical for performing well in sports, work and life. This book will teach you the essential mind-body skills for doing your absolute best in every aspect of life."
Alberto Salazar, Three-time winner, New York City Marathon

"Dr. Dahlkoetter's writing draws on a wealth of good illustrations both for motivation and for discovering your personal and athletic potential."
***Running Times Magazine,* Jonathan Beverly, Editor**

"This is a must read! I highly recommend this book to everyone who is pursuing excellence and deeper meaning in any area of their lives."
Misty Hyman, 2000 Olympic gold medalist, 200-M butterfly

"Great athletes are made, not born. This book explains where the training is done...between the ears."
Marty Liquori, world's #1 miler, NBC Olympics sports commentator; producer of ESPN's *Running and Racing*

"I'm convinced that mental training is as important to long term achievement and enjoyment in sports as the training of the muscles and the cardiovascular system."
Jeff Galloway, 1972 Olympian, 10,000 meters

"To make exercise a priority is an investment in your health, not an indulgence."
Katherine Switzer, 1974 New York City marathon champion

"I'm quite familiar with Dr. Dahlkoetter's work, seeing it regularly in several of the magazines that grace my mailbox. I especially like the use of specific examples in her writing. Much advice on sports psychology lacks this personal touch."
Joe Henderson, author of *Marathon Training*

"Dr. Dahlkoetter's writing on sports psychology contains sound information that can help athletes of all levels improve their training."
Scott Tinley, Two-time winner, Hawaii Ironman Triathlon

"My work with Dr. Dahlkoetter was essential in helping me prepare for the 2000 Olympic kayaking team. Her book puts into words what I always strive toward when I train and compete. She knows what it takes to get the best out of ourselves and move ahead with our lives."
Julia Sorzano, 2000 U.S. Olympic kayak team

"Working with many competitive athletes over the years, I recognize the significant role that mental training plays in performance. Dr. Dahlkoetter's book provides an exceptionally thorough and well thought out approach to mental training for athletes of all ability levels."
John K. Moore, D.C., C.C.N., Sydney 2000 - Chiropractor for U.S. Olympic swimmers; Chairman, International College of Applied Kinesiology Sports Council

"I compliment Dr. Dahlkoetter on her efforts in producing such a meaningful work for the betterment of others. Her excellent credentials, both athletic and academic, provide the foundation to write with confidence and experience."
Payton Jordan, 1968 Olympic track and field coach; former world record holder, 100 yards

"I've been reading Dr. Dahlkoetter's articles for several years and have found them very beneficial in my approach to mental training. Her book is a concise and easy-to-read compilation of her knowledge in the field of sports psychology that can help athletes improve their performance."
***Triathlete Magazine*, Lisa Lynam, contributing writer; Ironman triathlete; Canadian rowing champion**

"Dr. Dahlkoetter's advice was critical in helping me get ready for the 2000 Olympic Trials in single-handed sailing: *Your Performing Edge* will motivate you to move beyond your self-imposed limitations to achieve your best - A fantastic book!"
Krysia Pohl, 2000 U.S. Olympic trials qualifier, single-handed sailing

"*Your Performing Edge* is a compelling book, and it reads quite easily. She always provides solid, concrete examples of the items she's discussing, which most people have a hard time putting their finger on."
***Runner Triathlete News*, Lance Phegley, editor**

Your
PERFORMING
Edge

The Complete Mind-Body Guide
For Excellence in
Sports, Health and Life

JoAnn Dahlkoetter, Ph.D

Pulgas Ridge Press

Book Design by Geoffrey Faraghan, Telford Design
Cover Design by Anitra Nottingham, London Road Design

Library of Congress Control Number: 2001119301
ISBN 0-9704079-6-3

Printed in the United States of America
10 9 8 7 6 5 4 3 2

Published by Pulgas Ridge Press
        P.O. Box 730
        San Carlos,CA 94070-0730

Visit our Web Site: http://www.YourPerformingEdge.com
E-mail: info@sports-psych.com

Publisher's Note:
This book is written for educational purposes only and is not intended
for use as any type of psychotherapy or diagnostic instrument.

Library of Congress Cataloging-in-Publication Data

Dahlkoetter, JoAnn.
    Your Performing Edge : the complete mind-body guide
for excellence in sports, health and life / JoAnn Dahlkoetter.
--2nd ed.
    p. cm.
    ISBN 0-9704079-6-3

        1. Sports--Psychological aspects. 2. Success.
    3. Self-realization. 4. Athletes--Life skills guides.
    5. Athletes--Interviews. I. Title.

GV706.55.D34 2002
796'.01   2001119301

This book is for:

- My father for encouraging and nurturing the athlete in me. He knew it was a good thing for women to be strong and confident.

- My mother for bringing to life the psychologist in me. She is my best friend and confidant who has given me all the support and love I ever needed.

Contents

Foreword by

Bill Rodgers

JoAnn Dahlkoetter's book is what has been needed in the sports world for a long time, particularly for its emphasis on constructive step-by-step procedures that everyone can benefit from, but few understand.

Your Performing Edge provides the tools to develop confidence in yourself that will lead you to performing well. Can you imagine Michael Jordan or Tiger Woods not believing in himself? I know Dr. Dahlkoetter's techniques can make all of us better athletes and more successful in handling the stresses we find in our daily lives. She is not just promoting intellectual theories; she has been involved in top-level competition herself, in a wide variety of sports and serious athletic challenges. The fact that she has also produced countless successful athletes means a lot to me.

We have come a long way in our understanding of how to train the body for athletic success. Now, with Dr. Dahlkoetter's new book, we can go a step further by training the mind properly. I urge you to read this book if you wish to aim higher for yourself!

Foreword by

Joan Benoit Samuelson

JoAnn Dahlkoetter brings a wealth of knowledge and experience to the inside lane of the athlete's mind and body. Her background as a competitive athlete and her professional practice as a psychologist place her in a prime position to inspire and guide people to realize their true potential.

When Dr. Dahlkoetter came to speak at my running camp in Vermont, she gave a dynamic and perceptive presentation on sports psychology. Her new book now captures the essence of mental training in a concise and easy-to-read format that is filled with practical tools and exercises.

Dr. Dahlkoetter offers an uplifting, energetic, and enlightened approach to improving performance. She has a unique and encouraging style that makes learning a valuable and enjoyable experience. In *Your Performing Edge*, she shares a broad range of ideas, insights, and experiences that will help athletes and performers of all abilities to focus on their goals while achieving greater levels of success.

Acknowledgments

The creation of this book has been a long-term goal that would not have been possible without the support and assistance of many people at different stages from its origin to the final production.

I would like to give my sincere thanks to Bill Rodgers and Joan Benoit Samuelson for writing the foreword; to Geoff Faraghan, whose brilliant mind, computer expertise, and generosity played a major part in making this book possible; to, my graphic artist, Anitra Nottingham of London Road Design, for all her hard work, insights, and perseverance in designing the book cover; to Valarie Moore, for creating the logo and chapter symbols, and to Dan Poynter, my mentor, the wisest person I know in the book business.

I am grateful to the elite athletes and sports medicine professionals who participated in my interviews for this book: Lance Armstrong, Marion Jones, Dave Scott, Alberto Salazar, Mark Allen, Dan O'Brien, Stacy Dragila, Jeff Galloway, Marty Liquori, Scott Tinley, Katherine Switzer, Misty Hyman, Regina Jacobs, Payton Jordan, Grete Waitz, Carlette Guidry, and John Moore, D.C.

Many thanks to my principal book editors for their countless hours: Al Jacobs, Ph.D., Julie and Mike Dove, Elizabeth Fellows, and Marc Frodyma.

I feel fortunate to have had strong support from a number of magazine editors: Christina Gandolfo, editor of *Triathlete Magazine*; Jonathan Beverly, editor of *Running Times*; Beth Hagman and Marcos Cortez, editors of *Competitor Magazine,* Eileen Portz-Shovlin, senior editor of *Runner's World*; Lance Phegley, editor of *Runner Triathlete News*; Dave Stringer and Kees Tunsing, editors of *The Runner's Schedule*; Martin Rudow, editor of *Northwest Runner Magazine*; Claudia Piepenburg, editor of *Peak Running Performance*.

I appreciate the contributions from several excellent photographers: Graham Watson, for providing photos of Lance Armstrong; *Triathlete Magazine*, for its triathlon and running photos; Victah Sailor, for his photos from the 2000 Olympics; John Segesta, Randall Osterhuber; Lloyd Chambers, John Foss, and Albert and Dee Gaynor of Alpha CD Imaging.

Thank you also to my reviewers: Chuck and Sue MacDonald, Angela Fang, Jeffrey and Janice Fincher, Les and Noel Waddel, Robert Plant, Rick Campbell, Jim Ferstle, Lisa Lynam, Armen Khachadourian, Frank Smith, Nathan and Megumi Hoover, Chuck Wilson, Nancy Ikeda, Diane Palmason, Carol Langley, Karen Bivens, Brian Kirk, Pru Nelson, Al Rider, and Gail and Ernie Jones.

I wish to give a special thank you to William Dunn, for his photography expertise and creative eye, and his continual encouragement and support throughout the writing of this book.

And thanks to all of my clients over the years, who have taught me so much about life.

Preface

A passionate involvement in sports as an elite athlete and my experience as a performance consultant have provided me with a multidimensional perspective on performance. Through my 20 years of professional private practice and research, I have been able to absorb and reveal the collective wisdom of others. What I offer in this book is a reflection of my direct experience with athletes, coaches, and people in high stress professions striving to excel and improve the quality of their lives. Some of my clients have been Olympians, some have been serious life-long athletes, and some were just starting on their journey toward health and fitness. All have been dedicated to enhancing their level of performance and to discovering their true potential.

Valuable lessons come not only from one's own experiences, challenges, and triumphs but also from the stories and insights of others. It is gratifying to connect with people who truly commit themselves to improving their mental training skills. Athletes who commit to enhancing their mental discipline gain the greatest prize of all – the ability to live a higher quality of life. Through a series of extensive interviews this book contains the wisdom of many of the world's greatest athletes, including Lance Armstrong, Marion Jones, Dave Scott, Alberto Salazar, Mark Allen, Dan O'Brien, Stacy Dragila, Bill Rodgers Joan Benoit Samuelson, Jeff Galloway, Marty Liquori, Scott Tinley, Katherine Switzer, Misty Hyman, Regina Jacobs, Payton Jordan, Grete Waitz, and Carlette Guidry. I entered their worlds, grew from their insights, and have presented their stories in the chapters to follow.

The mission of this book is to be the complete mind-body-spirit guide for optimal performance in sports and in life. It is written to address performance issues for a wide range of sports and ability levels. The most effective tools and approaches discovered during my research and individual consultations are outlined in these chapters. I have provided clear guidelines with specific examples so that you can examine your own circumstances and goals, and then create a program that works for you.

Beyond pursuing excellence, I have found that sport teaches us countless lessons about how to live our lives. Thus, in addition to discussing athletic achievement, each section of the book also provides you with guidance on how to perform better in your personal and professional life. In doing so, this book provides the practical approach that is missing in many books on performance.

You'll find over 50 mental training exercises that allow you to practice and incorporate the strategies presented. This approach will accelerate and enhance the learning process, and will allow you to fully integrate these techniques into your daily life.

Beginning Your Journey: How Best to Use This Book

You are invited to read this book slowly and progressively, from beginning to end. Each chapter is a separate unit, however, so you can open the book any time and randomly choose a particular topic that is relevant to your needs. Each chapter uses a wide diversity of stories, illustrations, affirmations, and imagery exercises to help you integrate the concepts offered, and to fully train your mind and body for excellence. You are encouraged to take 10-15 minutes per day for practicing the techniques presented in order to turn your learning into action.

The book is divided into six parts, each of which contains chapters that reflect a particular theme. Part I, *Winning is a State of Mind*, establishes a foundation by presenting an enriched perspective of the route to success in sports and fulfillment in life. It goes beyond the traditional approach to sports psychology. You will learn that winning is not necessarily crossing a finish line or meeting a certain time goal. Winning is something that can happen deep within your heart, regardless of the external outcome. After evaluating a wide range of personal interviews from champion athletes, you'll be inspired and motivated to begin your personal journey to excellence.

In Part II, I build upon this framework to provide you with the *Essential Tools of the Trade* to become a more complete athlete with an integrated mind, body, and spirit. Learning the proper methods for doing breathing, imagery, affirmations, and goal setting will allow you to add a new mental dimension to your workouts while enjoying improved performance and personal satisfaction. These tools will become a vital part of your training routine.

In Part III, *The Optimal Performance Mindset* discusses various techniques to make the most of your mental and physical resources. You'll learn how to develop confidence and build a powerful self-image as an athlete. You'll acquire the art of mindfulness and of fine-tuning your concentration. More importantly, you'll understand what it takes to believe in yourself and your abilities.

In Part IV, *Performing with Intention*, you can use your new skills and apply them to the competitive arena. You'll read about handling pain, overcoming performance anxiety, and transcending limiting beliefs. You'll integrate all of the knowledge and experience you've gained, and put it all together on race day. You'll learn what it means to win, how to rebound from defeat, and how to evaluate your performance.

In Part V, *Obstacles as Vehicles for Healing*, I talk about the times of deep soul searching that come from setbacks in sports and in life. You'll learn about handling performance slumps, injuries, and burnout. You'll also become aware that healing takes place on many levels – both emotional and physical. I talk about how to manage difficult emotions and work through anger, grief, and depression.

Finally in Part VI, *Finding Meaning in Your Pursuits*, I put performance in perspective. I discuss how to create balance in your life and how to adjust your attitude during the aging process. I explain how a coach can help you understand the meaning of your athletic endeavors. You'll learn that sports can be a metaphor for everything you do and feel in life.

If the most creative and effective methods used by champion performers can be acquired and integrated into your life, then you can move forward, not only in the athletic arena, but also along the path of life. You can enjoy personal excellence and also have greater day-to-day fulfillment by using the strategies outlined in this book. I invite you to turn the page and discover *Your Performing Edge*.

Part
I

Winning
is a
State of Mind

Chapter
1

Discover
Your
True Potential

*"Anything is possible,
but you have
to believe
and you
have to fight"*

Lance Armstrong

Involvement in sports can be conceptualized as a personal journey that presents a wide variety of challenges for the body and mind. Most journeys have a predetermined destination and estimated time of arrival. However, when you begin your athletic voyage, regardless of age or ability level, the experience is one of continuous new beginnings - a lifetime of discovery and learning. The lessons may appear on many different levels - emotional, physical, and perhaps even spiritual - if you are open to them. As you evolve both athletically and personally, you'll discover that this voyage has no final destination. The purpose of traveling is for continual transformation and renewal as you keep refining the definition of what is possible.

Lance Armstrong is the definition of personal transformation, resiliency, and inner strength. He won the Tour de France, arguably the greatest bicycle race in the world, in 1999, 2000, and 2001, but even this accomplishment pales when compared to another victory he achieved earlier. In 1996 and '97 he fought the greatest battle of his life in overcoming testicular cancer. With only a 50 percent chance of living, Armstrong beat the odds, moving beyond mere survival to capture cycling's most prestigious crown.

Called the comeback athlete of the decade, Lance gave new hope to people who had all but given up in their own battles. With his second Tour de France win in 2000 and his bronze medal at the Olympics in Sydney, he was able to enjoy the victory while fully appreciating his extraordinary journey.

In athletics we encounter the full range of lessons and experiences that are needed to be successful in life. When you train and compete, you will eventually experience every conceivable emotional state, as you are compelled to respond to many demanding situations. The athletic arena is like a miniature play of life's trials, with all of the joys and hardships, progress and setbacks, success and shortcomings that we face in day-to-day living. Training becomes far more than physical activity or competition. It provides us with the perfect teaching ground for personal discovery and development.

Lance Armstrong knows about life's setbacks; he's a master at turning them into comebacks. In an interview just prior to the 2000 Olympics Lance said: "I owe all my victories to the cancer; this illness enabled me to win the Tour. Had I gotten just an early stage illness, I wouldn't be the same now. I would not have won the Tour de France two times. If I had not been through hell, I couldn't be here now."

Lance treated his cancer as aggressively as possible. He had brain surgery to remove tumors that temporarily blinded him. Then there were four rounds of the most potent chemotherapy treatment available to rid his body of a cancer that was out of control. After each session he would ride and try to understand why this was happening. He said: "I was mad at the illness. In sport you have competitors that are a little bit like the enemy. You have to put an enemy's face on them. So I tried to do that with the illness. I mean here you have something that was literally trying to take my life. I was pissed off that it chose me. So I tried to make it a fight – Lance versus the cancer.

"I had a lot of people that worked hard for my second life. I have a great family, and I met my wife through all of this. They have given me an awesome second life."

When Lance came to San Francisco for the Grand Prix cycling series in September of 2001, I had the opportunity to interview him. I said, "Lance, I know that coming back from cancer has made you mentally tough. How has that experience helped you stay positive in your training and racing?" He told me: "Whenever I feel like I'm having a bad day out there on the bike, I think back to Indianapolis in '96 and '97, when the cancer was in its worse stages, and that puts life into perspective. I realize that things aren't so bad. Coming from that experience, I can keep a positive outlook and handle any workout."

If you are to be successful in sports you are bound to develop those strategies and skills that are necessary to do well in other aspects of your life. For long-term accomplishment in athletics you need to learn determination, discipline, commitment, sacrifice, courage, mental toughness, confidence, and positive mental attitude. These are the primary skills that the majority of successful athletes exhibit in their training.

There is another part of training, however, that many people are missing. For personal satisfaction and growth you also need to develop those "softer qualities" of patience, humility, expression of feelings, faith in your plan, belief in yourself, accepting responsibility, and most importantly, a sense of enjoyment and fun. The good news is that these same abilities, once acquired in sports, are easily transferred into one's professional and personal life.

However, instead of creating joy and fun while developing potential, sports in our high stress competitive culture can often have a negative effect. Most athletes at some point experience tremendous pressure, fear, and anxiety produced by a strong compulsion to win. They become overly concerned with their time, score, or place - the external outcome - rather than receiving an inner sense of satisfaction from simply doing their best.

Common Concerns for Athletes

In my 20 years as a top endurance athlete and sports psychologist, I have worked with Olympic, professional, college, and recreational athletes of all ages in a wide range of sports. I have observed that regardless of ability level, the same kinds of problems arise: lack of motivation, self-doubt, stress and nervousness before races, low self-esteem, fear of recurring injuries, weight concerns, performance slumps, and lack of balance in one's life.

Athletes have particular difficulty with the issues listed below. Each of these concerns will be discussed in more depth in Sections III, IV, and V of this book:

External Orientation: Continually chasing tangible rewards and recognition rather than looking for inner fulfillment

Low Self-Esteem: Basing self-worth on performance and results alone rather than on a strong sense of personal identity

Unreasonable expectations: Setting unrealistic standards that lead to feelings of disappointment and failure

Self-Deprecation: Blaming oneself for mistakes and setbacks leading to anxiety and poor self-confidence

Results: Focusing primarily on the final outcome rather than on the actual process of one's training

Whether you've been preparing for an Olympic event, training to set a personal record, or working out for fun or fitness, there's an element of training you're probably neglecting. If the issues listed above sound familiar, you may not be putting an adequate amount of time into the psychological aspects of your training.

Mental preparation can do for the mind what stretching does for the body. It can make all the difference in how you experience your workouts and racing regardless of your fitness level or sport. Yet it is a skill that even the most conditioned athletes fail to practice sufficiently.

Just as we work out our bodies, we need to exercise the brain. Mental training is like taking your brain to the gym. We want our bodies to have many different gears and speeds. We also need the mind to be flexible, to shift into different gears, depending on the task at hand.

External or Internal Fix?

When I give professional seminars at corporations or clinics, people inevitably ask: "So what's the secret; what's the magic potion that's going to produce that quantum leap in performance?" Everyone is looking for an external fix: the special nutritional supplement, the rocketing gold track shoes of Michael Johnson, or the twelve-thousand-dollar bicycle of Lance Armstrong in the Tour de France.

You may be thinking: "If only Nike would design for me a pair of custom golden shoes maybe I could run a 19.32 world record in the 200 meters." They brought Michael the gold medals, right? However, if you took a good look into his eyes as he was warming up, stretching, approaching the starting blocks, and executing his events, you could appreciate his sense of unwavering focus, drive, and internal strength which brought him the results he was looking for. As Gail Devers said right before her Olympic 100-meter heat: "All I'm thinking about is what I have to do right now in this race. I'm just here to take care of business."

The good news is that you already have all the resources you need to produce the results and satisfaction you want. They are all right inside your head. It's just a matter of developing those mental skills as you have improved your physical endurance.

The Ethiopian medal count for running events at the 2000 Olympics demonstrates what is possible when athletes fully utilize their inner resources. The Ethiopians dominated the distance running events: first and third in the Men's Marathon; first and second in the Women's 10,000 meters; first and third in the Men's 10,000 meters; and first in the Men's 5,000 meters! In fact, the Ethiopian government declared a holiday for all employees to greet the athletes when they arrived home!

Imagine what would happen if the children of that country had access to running water, electricity, good nutrition, training facilities, serious coaching, and running shoes. Their potential is enormous in spite of their minimal resources. These achievements are based on sheer talent and incredible perseverance. The fact that the Ethiopians won so many Olympic distance races under these circumstances is astounding.

Could I Have a Major Breakthrough?

Let's say your next competition is two days away. No amount of physical training between now and then will make a significant improvement in the outcome (except of course over-training, which may well hinder your performance). However, the techniques that I will discuss in this book have the potential for creating a major breakthrough in both your workouts and in competitions. You can experience substantial growth as an athlete and have more fun and enjoyment as well. You'll learn to train smarter and with more intensity while reducing the risk of injury because you'll gain a new sensitivity to your body's signals. You can develop the ability to train with a sense of relaxed concentration so that your mind and body are 100% in the present moment, focusing solely on the task at hand. Then you'll tune in to a channel of energy that perhaps you've never before experienced, and broaden your perspective of what is possible.

Attributes of Top Performers

Take for example two people with similar physical capabilities (same maximum heart rate, bio-mechanical make-up, ratio of fast-twitch muscle fibers, etc.). One becomes an Olympian and the other ends up as a mediocre athlete, never making it beyond a few local competitions. Why do they perform so differently when they have virtually the same bodies? The answer lies in one's motivation and in using what one has to the fullest capacity.

Mental training techniques can help you bring back that joy and excitement for training and competition. You can develop a mindset of relaxed attention that allows you to open up to your greatest potential while enjoying the process of personal growth. You can develop a source of inner strength that you never knew existed. With mental training you can enhance your repertoire of tools and abilities so that you can respond effectively to the demands of any situation.

With proper training in sports psychology, using techniques such as confidence building, mindfulness, concentration, imagery, and goal setting, you can develop the qualities listed below. We'll be expanding on each of these issues in sections II through VI of this book:

Vision: Follow your passion; let your dreams unleash the exceptional powers of the body, mind, and spirit that will guide you to success in any activity.

Mental Flexibility: Become a multidimensional athlete with many ways of viewing a situation.

Self-understanding: Use sports to gain knowledge and foster personal growth.

Self-improvement: Assess your weaknesses and work toward changing them.

Balance: Strive for a healthy, harmonious lifestyle with time for a variety of pursuits.

Courage: Learn to handle adversity, take risks, learn from mistakes, and be able to move on to the next level.

Responsibility: Take charge of your own training, do your absolute best in racing, and accept your part in the outcome.

Resilience: Recognize that there will be inconsistencies in performance, and be able to weather both the good days and hard times.

Openness: Allow sports to set the platform for acquiring valuable lifelong lessons.

Enjoyment: Participate in a sport for the pure pleasure that it creates.

The greatest barriers in our quest to excel are the psychological ones that we impose on ourselves, often unconsciously. Whether it's the fear of a recurring knee pain, or going out too fast in the first mile of a triathlon, or hitting the wall at mile 20 of the marathon, or losing focus during the last mile of a bike ride, we all have mental or physical obstacles to overcome. With proper mental training you can learn to work through these blocks and enhance your motivation and self-confidence. You'll find that as your beliefs about your limits change, the limits themselves begin to shift. Beliefs give rise to reality.

The Integrated Athlete

You are a multidimensional person - a synthesis of body, mind, and spirit - capable of accomplishing extraordinary things. As you look through this book you'll begin to understand the many elements of the successful athlete and integrate a variety of components that complement one another. You'll find that you can be intellectual and emotional, energetic and relaxed, aggressive and sensitive, competitive and cooperative. All of these qualities can coexist in harmony in the same person.

The purpose of this book is to nurture and develop all of these attributes so that each part supports every other part of your being. It will help you to experience the broader, deeper elements of your sport. You will begin to comprehend the profound connection between your training and the subsequent changes in your heart and mind. You'll discover that your training is an interaction between your inner spirit and the natural environment around you.

Once these concepts are understood, you can then take the lessons from sport and allow them to enhance the way you think, feel, and behave in your everyday life. You'll become the complete athlete, who is also the focused student, the disciplined professional, or the nurturing parent. You can enjoy and appreciate the true value of the athletic lifestyle. This book will encourage and guide you to discover your true potential. So relax and get ready for a wonderful journey.

Chapter
2

Performing
Edge
Principles

*Go confidently
in the
direction
of your dreams*

Have you ever been totally in sync with the activity you were performing? Have you ever had the sense that, for a single moment, you were in complete control of your destiny? Have you ever felt such an intense pleasure in an action that you could continue doing it all day just for the experience, regardless of the outcome? The activity could involve completing a personal goal in a workout, or doing a brilliant presentation at work, or spending quality time with someone you care about. These types of occurrences make up the essence of your performing edge - those extraordinary moments when the mind and body are working together effortlessly, leaving you feeling that something special has just taken place. This state of consciousness has a multitude of well-known labels: peak performance, optimal experience, flow, and being in the zone. However you wish to portray this frame of mind, these experiences are certain to be connected to the most treasured moments in your lifetime.

I recently consulted with a runner on the U.S. track and field team who was training for the 2000 Olympics in Sydney. He described his peak experience in the Olympic Trials: "I felt strong and in control the whole time. Although the race was long, it seemed like I was in a time tunnel, with an endless source of energy. I was running faster than I ever had before, and yet it felt so easy.... with no pain or fear, just a sense of pure joy and excitement."

> I interviewed Stacy Dragila, world record holder and 2000 Olympic gold medalist in the pole vault. Just before the U.S. Olympic Trials in Sacramento, she related that: "Even when I enter a competitive event with an initial sense of nervousness, I turn that feeling into an expectation of success. I get this feeling of awesome power, an acute awareness, like there's nothing I can't do if I put my mind to it. It's a kind of knowing that comes from inside, that I can always jump higher."

Sports provide a variety of ways for athletes to experience optimal performance. People can feel this sense of control and power when they are winning a competition, setting a personal record, or just doing a morning workout. Yet this special state escapes many athletes; it appears mystifying and unattainable to most people. Many individuals encounter this state by chance and find it difficult to replicate. Indeed, some athletes work very hard for many years just to re-visit that ultimate feeling.

In contrast to the rest of life, athletics can offer a state of being that is so fulfilling one does it for no other reason than to be a part of it. These feelings are among the most intense, most remarkable ones we can obtain in this life. Once achieved, these optimal experiences remain engraved in the mind and supply the means to return to this state.

My studies and interviews with a wide variety of athletes over several years have established the framework for a better understanding of the performing edge state. Through this research, I have found several behavior patterns and attitudes that are clearly linked to the creation of this state. While achieving an optimal state of mind is not easy, this chapter describes how this ideal state can be achieved more often and identifies the conditions that allow it to occur.

Your Performing Edge Profile

What do athletes report during an optimal experience? This is a state of consciousness where a person becomes completely absorbed in the task at hand, to the exclusion of all other outside influences. You are totally focused on the present moment – the everyday world seems to recede into the background. During the peak experience you feel more self-assured and more fully integrated. Your mind, body, and spirit are tuned in to the moment. These are the times when you feel most energetic and fully alive.

Psychologist Abraham Maslow first studied individuals with peak experiences, called "self-actualizations," in the early 1960s. He researched human behavior at its most personally fulfilling levels. He found that during peak experience "the human powers come together in a particularly efficient and intensely enjoyable way.... in which the person is more open to experience, more expressive or spontaneous, fully functioning, more truly oneself, more fully human."

> One top triathlete I coached recently noted that during his best event: "It was like I was in an invisible envelope where the only thing that existed was this race. I was essentially unaware of myself.... like my body was being directed from an unconscious part of myself, rather than by my thoughts. I did not have to think about each move.... I was on automatic pilot."

An equestrian athlete talked about her performing edge: "I remember my best show at Pebble Beach. I could remain focused and relaxed no matter what happened. I was able to manage my nerves. I recall moving toward the first set of fences, riding clean, conservatively at first. Then I got into a rhythm; it felt smooth. For each of the turns I was helping the horse get into the best spot; I kept him moving forward. The moment we were in the air, I was looking for the next fence. I was becoming more comfortable going faster and faster. I wasn't afraid of the speed. I just went with my instincts; my body seemed to know exactly what to do. The quality of jumping was so good. My horse was jumping two feet over the fence, yet it felt effortless."

During these moments the athlete focuses on the precise details of the event that allow him or her to respond optimally. Athletes often report intense concentration on a small action – passing a competitor on the bike or finding just the right swimming form. People speak of the unusual sense of stepping into a heightened state of awareness. Sometimes there is a keen sense of "the big picture," where a person says: "I could almost tell exactly how the next play would develop, and I could anticipate the correct moves to handle the situation."

> Brigette McMahon, from Switzerland, gold medalist in the 1st Olympic triathlon, said: "I used the same tactics in Sydney as I did at the World Championships. I knew the course well. I had a relaxed focus. I could sense every move and I knew exactly when to attack and take control of the race."

Athletes also report a feeling of power during optimal performance that transcends their usual level of strength and energy. This outpouring of power is often apparent to other athletes or spectators. When people watched the eyes of Mark Allen in the marathon section of the Hawaii Ironman Triathlon, they reported: "He looks so driven, so consumed by the momentum of the race itself, that nothing can stop him." The activity itself takes over and the individual feels completely synchronized within it.

Misty Hyman, 2000 Olympic gold medalist in the 200 meter butterfly, talked about her performing edge experience:

"For some reason at the Olympics I said, OK, I'm not going to try to control this. I'm going to allow it to happen. So I walked in there and just relaxed, and said OK, I can do this.

"Everything went so smoothly. I don't remember the events of the finals exactly. I know that I was definitely in the moment, and I wasn't thinking too much. I was doing what I needed to do.

"I remember feeling nervous while going through my warm-ups. I felt different than I ever had before. Things would just happen naturally when I would get in the water. Even though I wasn't thinking about my stroke, I would just do things correctly without really trying. My body would just take over.

"When standing on the blocks, I just said to myself, Ok, I'm going to do a 200 butterfly, and I've done a million 200 butterflies in my life. I have been training for this and I know exactly what I need to do. I remember being able to feel every cell in my body and be completely present. Things felt like they were in slow motion. I dove in the water and it just clicked. I felt more power than ever before."

One key characteristic of the optimal experience, perhaps the best of all, is a sense of sheer ecstasy or joy. Although a peak performance or personal record is desirable, the optimal experience does not depend on it. One athlete I worked with recalled her feelings swimming in the ocean as a child: "I developed an emotional and physical attraction to the water and the simple joy of movement." When she finally completed her swim across the San Francisco Bay in the Escape from Alcatraz triathlon, she related: "There is no amount of wealth, no position in life that can equal that experience. It's not the prize at the finish line that counts. It's doing an activity that is totally pure and experiencing an ideal state of well-being."

Whenever athletes describe their peak performances, similar images tend to emerge, as they relate what happens internally. One top athlete summed up what many athletes feel as she related her experience during an extraordinary performance:

"The morning air was crisp and clear, just like my thoughts and feelings. I felt very calm, but energized and focused at the same time. I was optimistic about doing well that day, but I wasn't concerned about the outcome. As soon as the event was underway, the fear and anxiety subsided, and I felt quiet inside. All my actions seemed to flow effortlessly. I did not have to decide about what to do next; it all just happened so naturally.

"Even though I was moving very fast, I had a sense that this was the right pace. I seemed to have enough time to complete each action without hurrying. Sometimes it felt like I was in a time tunnel, as if things were in slow motion. I felt strong and powerful, like there was nothing I could not do. My confidence was at an all-time high. I felt invincible. I was in total control.

"This heightened awareness made it easy to concentrate and be in the moment. I felt really tuned in to the task at hand. All that mattered was what I was doing at that time. The outside distractions just faded into the background, as I focused my attention solely on what was happening and what was about to happen. It was intense, and yet fun at the same time. The whole experience was so exhilarating and enjoyable."

In my work with athletes I have found that maintaining this type of internal climate is critical for performing well and for producing an enjoyable experience. Playing well is a natural outcome of having the right kind of internal feelings. When you feel good, your training improves. Your level of performance is a direct reflection of the way you think and feel. Thus, to produce an optimal performance you need to create and sustain the right type of internal climate regardless of what is going on around you.

Athletes' Expressions for the Optimal Experience:

"Strong and powerful"   "Effortless speed"
"Physically relaxed"   "On automatic pilot"
"Calm and at peace"   "No fear or anxiety"
"Mentally focused"   "Feeling invincible"
"Light and fluid"   "Total self-confidence"
"Optimistic and positive"   "Floating with ease"
"Tuned in to the moment"   "Completely engaged"
"Acute awareness"   "Detached from the outcome"
"Natural and spontaneous"   "In perfect control"
"Fun and enjoyable"   "Ideal sense of well-being"
"Embracing the task at hand"   "In the zone"
"Energized"   "Everything falls into place"
"Absolute composure"   "Fully alive"

I asked two-time Ironman winner Scott Tinley to describe his greatest moment as a triathlete. Surprisingly, it was not his victories in 1982 and 1985. He said: "The race that meant the most to me was the 1981 Ironman when I placed third. I did not have any expectations. I was not hoping for a certain place or time and so I didn't put any pressure on myself. I just told myself, it is what it is."

The mind and body are so well connected that it becomes difficult to achieve a good outcome when the proper mindset is not present. The right internal state must be created first. Once you feel right inside, a quality performance can occur naturally and effortlessly. The appropriate internal state can bridge the gap between what you think you can accomplish and what you actually achieve. It can make the difference between having the ability and realizing your true potential.

Marion Jones said in an interview before the 2000 Olympics: "As a child, I was a tomboy.... never owned a doll in my life. I was always outside playing sports. I had this sense that something of greater proportions was going to occur in my life." Before Sydney, Marion felt she had the ability to win five medals at the Olympics. During the opening ceremonies she was taking home videos, laughing, and smiling. She was learning to balance the pressure with fun. Developing a belief in herself and creating the right internal atmosphere allowed her to come away with those five medals. She completed the connection between her vision and reality.

Key Characteristics of the Performing Edge State

> A focus on the present moment that is so intense actions can often be foreseen before they occur.

> A sense of unusual power that appears to come from an outside source or from a new source within oneself.

> A feeling of being totally immersed in an activity, being completely in tune with the task at hand.

> An expectation that one has the ability to meet the challenge ahead.

> A perception that the past and future seem to fade away as the present action is the only thing that matters.

> A sense of total joy and elation, a harmonious experience of mind, body, and spirit.

The performing edge is a state that can be experienced by anyone in a wide range of contexts. We'll be discussing more specific techniques for developing your edge in sections II and III. Use the affirmations below to allow this type of experience to occur more often in your training and competition.

Your Performing Edge Affirmations
Try repeating these phrases before your next event.
  I feel a sense of power and strength from within.
  I stay positive and optimistic no matter what happens.
  I am tuned into what I am doing each moment.
  I fully enjoy every part of my workout.
  I project confidence and energy.
  I am physically relaxed and mentally focused.
  I am in my element; I am fully engaged in this activity.

Chapter
3

Creating
an
Inner Desire

*Look around you,
find your passion,
see what makes
you whole*

To excel as an athlete you must be hungry - hungry for success, for results - hungry simply to become the best athlete you can be. It starts with a dream, but somehow you must be inspired or you will never be able to reach your goal. We often read about athletes overcoming physical disabilities. Lance Armstrong survived testicular cancer and won the Tour de France two times. Marla Runyan ran in the 1500 meters of the 2000 Olympics while being legally blind. It is out of these challenges that athletes develop a fierce, burning desire to succeed. They need to prove to themselves that they can achieve their goals. Through these kinds of examples we can begin to understand that desire is sometimes more important than even talent or a healthy body.

> The movie "Prefontaine" depicts the life of a running legend who had one leg shorter than the other and did not necessarily have "the perfect runner's body." Yet from a very early age he developed an insatiable love for running. Through his drive and determination Steve Prefontaine went on to break the American record in every distance from 2,000 - 10,000 meters, a feat never attained by any other American man.

Without a true love for your sport and a burning desire to be the best you can be, you will never be able to push yourself to do what has to be done. It will be too easy to skip a workout now and then. A coach or parent can give you support and guidance, but you have to supply the rest. Only you can push yourself when you're tired or make yourself work out when distractions get in the way. After Steve Prefontaine had reached the height of his running career, he lost to Lasse Viren in the Olympic 5,000 meters in Munich. The loss led him to consider quitting the sport. His coach, Bill Bowerman, told him: "If you're gonna run, be at the track and I'll give you the workouts; or if you're gonna stop running, then do that. You decide. I can't coach desire."

So the drive must come from within, regardless of whether you're a novice, a serious athlete, or a competitor at the elite level. The good news is that building and maintaining a high level of self-motivation is a learned skill that anyone can acquire. Motivation is energy, and that sense of self-directedness is one of the most powerful sources of energy available to an athlete. From internal motivation you gain the willingness to persevere with your training, to endure discomfort and stress, and to make sacrifices with your time and energy as you move closer toward realizing your goal.

Profile of the Highly Motivated Athlete

What are the key characteristics of well-motivated athletes? Through my extensive work with numerous athletes over several years, I have developed a constellation of traits that defines the champion's mentality. Elite athletes do not possess superhuman powers or extraordinary qualifications limited to a select few. The characteristics that make a champion can be attained and developed by anyone who wants to excel in a sport.

Enthusiasm and desire - love for your sport: Top athletes have a hunger, a fire inside which fuels their passion to achieve an important goal, regardless of their level of talent or ability. To accomplish anything of value in life you need to begin with some kind of vision or dream. The more clearly you can see that picture in your mind, the more likely it is to become reality. Wherever you place your attention, your energy will follow.

Courage to succeed: Once an athlete has the desire, he or she needs to back it up with courage - the incentive to make any dream you dare to dream become reality. It takes courage to sacrifice, to work out when you're tired, to seek out tough competition when you know you'll probably lose. It takes courage to stick to your game plan and the relentless pursuit of your goal when you encounter obstacles. It takes courage to push yourself to places that you have never been before – physically or mentally. It takes courage to test your limits and to break through barriers.

Internal motivation and self-direction: Champion athletes decide early on that they are training and competing for themselves, not for their parents, their coaches, or the medals. Direction and drive need to come from within. The goals must be ones that you have chosen because that's exactly what you want to be doing. Ask yourself, what keeps you training? Whom are you doing it for?

Commitment to excellence: How good do you want to be? Elite athletes know that to excel at their sport, they must decide to make it a priority in their life. They make an honest effort each day to be the best at what they do. At some point you must say, I want to be really good at this; I want this to work. To notice significant growth, you must live this commitment and regularly stretch what you perceive to be your current limits.

Discipline, consistency, organization: Winning athletes know how to self-energize and work hard on a daily basis. Because they love what they do, it is easier for them to maintain consistency in training and in competing. Regardless of personal problems, fatigue, or difficult circumstances, they can generate the optimal amount of excitement and energy to do their best.

Being focused and yet relaxed: Champions have the ability to maintain concentration for long periods of time. They can tune in what's critical to their performance and tune out what's not. They can easily let go of distractions and take control of their attention.

Ability to handle adversity: Top athletes know how to deal with difficult situations. Adversity builds character. When elite athletes know the odds are against them, they embrace the chance to explore the outer limits of their potential. Rather than avoiding pressure, they feel challenged by it. They are calm and relaxed under fire. Setbacks become an opportunity for learning; they open the way for deep personal growth.

> Dan O'Brien, Olympic gold medalist in the decathlon, knows about handling adversity. During my interview with him he recalled: "When I didn't make the opening height for the pole vault in the 1992 Olympic Trials, there was no doubt in my mind where I was going. Sure I was upset, but I dealt with it and quickly moved on. That event set the pace for the next four years of my training. I was driven. I knew I could be the best. I surrounded myself with people who shared that same vision. I wrote my goals down on paper so I could see them every day."
>
> Only six weeks after the Olympic Trials Dan shattered the world record in the decathlon at the Deca Star Meet in Tolance, France. He went on to become the 1996 Olympic Decathlon Champion in Atlanta. Adversity fueled his vision. Dan says: "If you can see it, you can achieve it."

Building Desire and Motivation

The people who develop these qualities and practice these skills regularly have the best chance of excelling athletically as well as personally and professionally. Each of us begins at a different starting point physically and mentally. We all have strengths that we can build upon. Now that you have an idea of the constellation of traits that successful athletes possess, how do you begin to build them into your life? How do you turn these qualities into useful behaviors that will make a difference in the way you train and race? Numerous researchers in the sports psychology field have reported on the critical skills and behaviors of successful athletes. Below I have offered suggestions that have helped many of my own clients tremendously toward excelling in their sport.

Generate a positive outlook: Direct your focus to what is possible, to what can happen, toward success. Rather than complaining about the weather or criticizing the competition, the mentally trained athlete attends to only those things that he or she can control. You have control over your thoughts, your emotions, your training form, and your perception of each situation. You have a choice in what you believe about yourself. Positive energy makes peak performances possible.

Visualize your goals daily: Put yourself in a relaxed state through deep abdominal breathing. Then, as vividly as possible, create an image in your mind of what you want to achieve in your sport. You can produce a replay of one of your best performances in the past. Then use all those positive feelings of self-confidence, energy, and strength in your mental rehearsal of an upcoming event. See yourself doing it right. Then use your imagery during the event itself.

© Julia Sorzano

Practice being focused and yet relaxed: Develop the ability to maintain concentration for longer periods of time. You can tune in what's critical to your performance and tune out what's not. You can easily let go of distractions and take control of your attention. As you focus more on the task at hand (e.g., your training form, how you're feeling), there will be less room for the negative thoughts to enter your mind.

Build a balanced lifestyle: Create a broad-based lifestyle with a variety of interests; strive for a balance between work and fun, social time, personal quiet time, and time to be creative. Develop patterns of healthy behavior. Eat regularly, get a consistent amount of sleep each night, reduce your work load at times if possible, and allow time to relax and reflect between activities. Develop a social support network of close friends and family, some who are sports oriented, and some with other interests. Learn to communicate openly; resolve personal conflicts as they occur so they don't build to a crisis on the night before an important race.

© John Segesta – Triathlete Magazine

Vary your workouts: Train at a new, scenic place at least once a week. Change your normal training schedule, even if only for two days. Try "active rest" by doing a different sport for a few days (e.g., hiking, swimming, inline skating, cycling, or cross-country skiing). You'll get a tremendous psychological boost and probably not lose any of your fitness level. Put new spark in your training schedule by doing interval work, tempo work (fast 20-30 minute training), or fartlek training (variable speeds), rather than slogging along at the same old pace.

Enjoy and take the pressure off: Make a deliberate effort each day to create enjoyment in your sport, renewing your enthusiasm and excitement for training. Don't try to force your physical improvement. Lighten up on your rigid training schedule and exercise according to your feelings each day. Remove the strict deadlines and race dates which have been cast in stone. Let your next breakthrough occur naturally, at its own pace, when the internal conditions are right. Use setbacks as learning opportunities. Do the best that you can do, draw out the constructive lessons from every workout and race, and then move on. Look for advantages in every situation, even if the conditions are less than ideal.

Sport offers a wonderful chance to free ourselves for short periods and experience intensity and excitement not readily available elsewhere in our lives. In endurance sports we can live out our quest for personal control by seeking out and continuously meeting challenges that are within our capability. To develop an inner desire and maximize your true potential, make the most of the talents you have and stretch the limits of your abilities, both physically and psychologically. Athletics can become a means to personal growth and enjoyment of the pursuit of your goals.

In my personal interview with Alberto Salazar, three-time winner of the New York City Marathon, I asked him about his perspective on running and life. He told me, "When I coach high school kids, I try to convey to them is that winning a race is not nearly as important as the lessons they take from their training and racing experience. They can transfer their confidence, self-discipline, and perseverance from sports directly into the rest of their lives."

Try incorporating the profile above into your mental preparation, and you can learn to live more fully, train more healthfully, and feel exactly the way you want to feel.

Positive Affirmations for Creating Desire

Now try repeating each of these positive affirmations two times:

- ➤ I believe in myself, I radiate an inner confidence.
- ➤ I am fully focused and self-directed during my workouts.
- ➤ I am strengthening my motivation and drive every day.
- ➤ I am becoming better friends with my body.
- ➤ I like myself more and more each day.
- ➤ I see steady improvement in physical fitness and strength.

MISTY DAWN HYMAN - U.S.A. - GOLD
SYDNEY 2000 - 200 BUTTERFLY - 2:05.88 - O.R.

Chapter
4

An Inside View
of the
2000 Olympics

*Sports is the
complete metaphor
for comprehending
all of life's
challenges*

M isty Hyman, a student at Stanford University, pulled off one of the biggest upsets of the 2000 Olympic games with her gold medal swim in the 200-meter butterfly. This is the event that people will remember for decades. Confident, calm, and in the moment, Misty accomplished the unthinkable. She beat Australia's "Madam Butterfly," who had been undefeated for six years. Misty beat Suzie O'Neil, the world record holder, in her best event on her home turf. In the process she swam 2:05:88, setting new Olympic and American records and clocking the 2nd fastest time in history.

I had the opportunity to interview Misty just two months after her Olympic gold medal swim.

JoAnn Dahlkoetter: It sounds like you've been very busy since you got your gold medal in Sydney.

Misty Hyman: Yes, during the week after my event I was on the Today Show four times, then I was on Good Morning America, followed by an interview with Bob Costa. Shortly after the Olympics, the swim team got to visit the White House and meet the President. And just last week the Olympic gold medalists were honored at the *Sports Illustrated* Athlete of the Year Awards in New York. I got to meet Tiger Woods, talk with Michael Johnson, and ride in a limousine with Sugar Ray Leonard. Lance Armstrong was honored with an award as well.

JD: What was the road to the Olympics like for you? Were there mental hurdles that you had to overcome?

MH: Oh, definitely! We arrived in Sydney three weeks prior to the competition. The Olympic Village was overwhelming; there was so much energy. *Sports Illustrated* would put on these wonderful parties. You'd see athletes from so many countries. It was exciting and yet tiring. There would be those self doubts that would come up. "Am I good enough? What am I made of? Do I belong here?"

Being in Sydney was frustrating at times. When you're back at home everything happens like clockwork. When you get to the Village, you're out of your normal routine. There's a loss of control. There was a lot of waiting around. You have to take buses everywhere. You know you're in a team setting. You have to make a lot of decisions based on other people's schedules.

We were lucky to have people like Dr. John Moore, our team chiropractor. There was a set-up called the High Performance Center. That was where the U.S. team people had a massage staff, physical therapists, and sports medicine doctors. In the past you didn't have a facility to meet with those types of people.

JD: Take me through your experience two days before your race.

MH: The first couple of days after I arrived in the Village, I ended up twisting my ankle, just walking down the stairs. So I was limping around for a while and had to miss a practice. I was really nervous about that. I couldn't believe it. That was a week before my event. They taped up my ankle. But it was a little thing, maybe just nerves. But that gradually went away.

Then the day before the opening ceremonies I came down with a 24-hour Australian flu bug. I was completely out of it. I was really tired with a bad stomach ache. So I ended up sleeping for 18 hours one day, going on a new anti-flu medication, and not being able to eat for a day. Because of that, I decided not to march in the opening ceremonies. I think that was a good decision, because there would be a lot of walking, and I would have to stay up late.

The swimming events start on the first day of the Olympics. So it's always a big decision whether or not to be in the opening ceremonies. I'm glad I made that decision, but it was so hard to watch it on TV, being so close to the event and not being able to go. The greatest thing was every morning I could wake up and look out my window and see the Olympic torch. It was so beautiful. I would get the chills each day, just gazing at it. I would think, I can't believe I'm here. It was just like a dream come true.

JD: Did you ask yourself, "Am I going to be well enough for the race?"

MH: Absolutely. My coach, Richard Quick, had to give me a big pep talk. A lot of decisions had to be made there. And when you're facing something that big, every little decision becomes huge. I had spent all summer doing everything I possibly could to prepare for the event. So when it came down to the final few days, every decision I made seemed so crucial. I probably blew it out of proportion.

So while I was recovering from the flu, Richard said, "You know, this isn't going to set you back. You're in good enough shape; you've done everything you can for this event. You've got plenty of time to recover." But I was really questioning myself. When you're at the Olympics, you try to control everything, yet you can't control all the variables.

Looking back, I had also been on antibiotics all summer because of an illness I had contracted earlier. In May of this year I got a multi-layered sinus infection. There was fluid in my lungs. When it was diagnosed, I almost had to quit swimming completely. So I'm thinking, "Am I falling apart, or am I gonna get myself together here?"

My event was on the fourth night of the meet. The timing was perfect. Every night we would go to the meet, and I would watch my teammates swim. There's something special about being on the U.S. team. There is a certain energy about the team, a camaraderie, a spirit, a synergy that's so powerful. I think that's one of the keys to our success. There is something special about wearing the red, white, and blue. You are out there, and you know why you are doing this. Everybody wants you to do well. When you look at your teammates up in the stands and they're cheering for you, there's a unique kind of power that really can make a difference. I would come home every night and be walking on air.

When you're watching your teammates down there, you know that they are the people you're going to see at the village that night. Yet it still seems like you're watching a movie. The sound was so amazing, 18,000 people cheering. For swimming that's pretty incredible.

JD: Tell me about the night before your race.

MH: On the night before my race, it took me about an hour to fall asleep. I remember I had to keep reassuring myself. I'd say I know what I need to do, I don't need to question myself. I had to have that core belief in myself and have the courage to just let it all go.

The qualifying actually takes place over two days. They have the prelims and the semi-finals on the first day. Then, the finals are the following night. During the prelims I was very relaxed. I knew that even despite a sprained ankle and being sick, in the summer leading up to the Olympics I had the best training camp of my life. I had some training times that were absolutely unbelievable, breakthroughs like I had never seen before. Then after the trials, I made even more improvements. So I had that confidence to build on. That made a huge difference. Every day the coaches would say, "I've never seen anybody do what you did today."

Dennis Pursley is the national team director. He used to coach Mary T. Meagher. She held the World records for butterfly. She's the one whose Olympic and American records I broke. He used to train her, and he said, "Mary never could have done what you just did today." She was the legendary Madam Butterfly because she held the 100 and 200-meter butterfly world records since 1981. They were the longest held world records in swimming. Nobody had even come close until 1998. Then Suzie O'Neil broke her 200 butterfly WR, and Jenny Thompson broke her 100 butterfly WR.

So that was really special for me to hear that feedback leading up to the Olympics. I knew that my body was ready. Actually I think the illness may have been a blessing in disguise. One of the biggest keys to me doing well was that. So maybe those things happened for a reason. I realized I needed to sleep for 18 hours. Without being sick I wouldn't have let myself do that.

I remember feeling nervous while going through my warm-ups. I felt different than I ever had before. Things would just happen naturally when I would get in the water. Even though I wasn't thinking about my stroke, I would just do things correctly without really trying. My body would just take over.

I remember every time I would walk into that ready room, before going on deck, I'd just get into 'the zone.' I would just be relaxed. For some reason at the Olympics I said, "OK, I'm not going to try to control this. I'm going to allow it to happen." So I walked in there and just relaxed, and said, "OK, I can do this."

JD: So you didn't let your head get in the way.

MH: Exactly. So I didn't get up on the blocks thinking I'm at the Olympics, there's 18,000 people, this is the biggest race of my life. Instead of building it up like that I said, "OK, this is a swim meet, I've done all that I can to prepare, I'm just going to go out there and have fun."

JD: Take me through each race. What was your mental state like during the prelims?

MH: In the prelims I was pretty relaxed. I took two seconds off my best time. My previous best time was 2:09:20. I swam 2:07:60 in the prelims and qualified first for the semis. I felt so smooth, relaxed, and within myself. I got really excited when I saw my time. People were saying, "Misty, it's just the prelims, you're not supposed to go that fast." I was cheering like I had won the gold medal. Going into the race, I had no idea how I would place. Then, taking two seconds off my best time, how can you argue with that?

JD: Were you more nervous in the semi-finals?

MH: Definitely, I was a little more nervous. I was saying, "I don't know if I can do it again. Was that just a fluke? Did I already use everything up in the prelims? Now I've set myself up for people expecting me to go that fast."

I like to warm up for my event really close to the time that I march out for the race. We have these new Speedo fast skin suits made from a new material. They are full body suits that are faster than shaved skin.

The night of the semi-finals I was nervous. Richard said, "You need to get over there. They're waiting for you in the ready room." I ran to the bathroom to put on my fast suit. When I pulled it up, a big hole ripped up the side of my suit. It was huge; I was screaming, "This is the semi-finals of my only Olympic race!"

So I took the suit off and threw it in the garbage. Richard ran and got me a second suit. So I'm saying, "Stay calm, keep my composure, don't use up all my energy." But I'm thinking, they're going to start the race without me. You know, being in the zone is really important, and at that point I kind of lost it.

Then when I finally got my suit on and was ready to go, there were long TV delays. So I ended up sitting in the ready room for 20 minutes. Now I was actually nervous about not being warmed up enough instead of about getting there in time.

They announced our event and I got up on the blocks. I managed to get it together enough to swim the race. Richard and I both knew that I was not in my optimal mental state. So the fact that I swam a 2:07 again while not in the perfect state, and I was able to pull it off by sheer will gave me a lot of confidence.

JD: Were you thinking, can I go even faster in the finals?

MH: Yes. I was pretty excited about the possibilities. The night before the race I slept pretty well because I was tired from swimming two races. The next morning I slept in, had breakfast, and went to the pool. I remember stretching and packing a towel in my bag. I noticed I was shaking, thinking I can't believe this is actually the finals of the Olympics.

MISTY DAWN HYMAN - U.S.A. - GOLD
SYDNEY 2000 - 200 BUTTERFLY - 2:05.88 - O.R., A.R.

© Misty Hyman

JD: Did you do anything the night before your race to help you get ready mentally?

MH: I visualized my race. I like to visualize my kick count and walk through my race in my head. I always count my kicks underwater so I have an idea of how many strokes I want to do on each length. I would visualize what I was going to think about on the blocks. I remember thinking I just really wanted to start the race. There had been so much anticipation for this one moment. Like let's just get to the punch line. I remember that night before the race I ate dinner alone. I actually ate a lot, since I'm an emotional eater. I remember eating way too much, but I was thinking, I have to have enough fuel. I felt very introverted. I really didn't want to talk to anybody or see anybody. Then I listened to some of my favorite songs. I always listen to the Sting song "Fields of Gold" before I go to bed.

JD: What was your mental set like going into the finals?

MH: Everything went so smoothly. I don't remember the events of the finals exactly. I know that I was definitely in the moment, and I wasn't thinking too much. I was doing what I needed to do. I was accepting the fact that I'm at the Olympics. I was telling myself I know how to do this.

I remember getting into the ready room. That was when I finally relaxed. My friend and teammate Katlin was with me the whole time. She was in the lane right next to me in the race. We were just joking around. When we walked out onto the deck, I remember slapping hands with her. I remember just smiling and thinking this is fun. I waved to the 18,000 people. I could see the team USA banner up there. They were cheering for us. I'm usually pretty tense during that moment before a race. But for some reason I was the most relaxed that I've ever been in my life.

I walked out there and I was thinking, all right, I'm going to show you what I can do. This is what I love. I'm going to just show the world what's inside me, what I've been doing every day of my life, and what is such a huge part of me.

One of my favorite movies is *The Cutting Edge*. It's about a figure skater and hockey player who are doing pairs skating. They end up winning a gold medal in the Olympics. Right before they start their competition, the woman says, 'I'm in the mood to kick a little ass.' It's a movie that has always inspired me.

When I marched out to the pool to swim the final race, they were actually playing a song from that movie. It was so perfect. I walked up onto the blocks and said to myself, "I'm in the mood to kick a little ass." I was laughing at myself that I could actually say that. I thought I'm just going to have fun out there. I'm going to do it.

My Dad was in the stands watching me. He said to me later, "I haven't seen you that relaxed in a very long time. I knew you were going to do well. You were smiling on the starting blocks." Richard laughed because I was the last one off the blocks when the gun went off. I told him I was too busy smiling. The amazing thing is that I was not even thinking about the fact that this was the Olympic finals. I wasn't thinking at all about Suzie O'Neil. I wasn't thinking about the fact that I was swimming in front of the whole world.

I just said to myself, "Ok, I'm going do a 200 butterfly; I've done a million 200 butterflies in my life. I have been training for this and I know exactly what I need to do." I remember being able to feel every cell in my body and be completely present. Things felt like they were in slow motion. I dove in the water and it just clicked.

In the past I would sometimes have too much tension in my body or put too much effort out in the beginning of the race. There are so many things to be concerned with. You just have to hit that right balance between effort and flow. And there's a certain rhythm especially for a 200 butterfly. It's such a long race you really have to manage all your energy. It's not something you can think about, it's more the sort of thing you just have to let happen.

So as I dove in, I remember feeling the cold water. I could feel how the water was flowing smoothly on my brand new suit. I remember looking down and thinking, Oh, I'm actually in the lane where the underwater camera is. Instead of forcing my arms with each stroke, they were just flowing. It's not like I was making anything happen. I just stayed in that zone the whole time. I don't think I knew exactly where the other competitors were in the race. I remember counting my kicks and strokes.

It's definitely a mental thing. In the Olympic Trials I fell apart mentally by using too much energy at the beginning. Typically I would take out the first 100 very quickly and then not be able to hold on. I'm often first to the 100, first to the 150 sometimes, but rarely first to the finish. If you get too mentally greedy, to try and get it all now, you end up using up too much energy too early. I needed to have the courage to trust myself on that last turn, and know that I could be strong enough to the finish without allowing that wall to hit. I needed to keep pushing that wall away.

In the Olympic final, for the first time in my career I said, "I know I can make it home. I know I can finish this." I said, "Nothing is going to stop me." It was that last turn that made such a difference. I really gained on the field. And that's right where I knew I was going to be able to do it.

JD: Did you know at that point that you could win the race?

MH: On the final lap I didn't actually know that I was winning. But I realized that all the pieces had finally come together. The moment I hit the wall, I knew I had just swum the best race of my life. It was amazing that I didn't feel tired at all. I had to look up at the scoreboard three times. I saw the #1 by my name, but it took a while for it to register. I hadn't really thought about the outcome. I was so wrapped up in executing my race. Then, I asked myself, "OK, number one, what does that mean? That means I just got first at the Olympics; that means I actually won the gold medal!" My teammate Katlin yelled, "You did it, you did it!" The crowd was actually silent for a long time. It was such a big upset. Everyone expected Suzie O'Neil to win. Finally I recognized I had won. Then I started screaming and smiling. The whole night I was walking on air.

It had been such a long build-up for so many years. So much went into creating the stage for this to happen. All the difficult challenges and hard work that had led up to that moment flashed through my mind. I mean, what are the chances of that happening, to have that one breakthrough race come together on the night that it's supposed to? There are some variables you can regulate, but there are so many that you can't control. I felt a very special energy that night. I remember seeing the American Record on the scoreboard and realizing that I had just beat Suzie O'Neil. It was almost too much for me to grasp. Suzie hadn't lost a race in six years. She was defending Olympic Champion and world record holder. She is basically their national hero. There are 10 x 10 foot billboards of her face everywhere downtown. She is like the Michael Jordan of Australia. Everyone expected her to win.

The best part for me was that I really felt comfortable in my own skin. A lot of times world class athletes feel like they have something to prove or there is an image that they have to live up to. There's a certain idea of what Olympians are like, and people are always trying to live up to that. But this time I finally let go, and I was completely myself. I was honest with what I was feeling. I felt like there was no wall between me and anyone else.

JD: What was the awards ceremony like for you?

MH: The ceremony was immediately after the event. It was amazing. Ever since I was a little girl, I would go to the swim meets. They would start the meet with the national anthem. I would put my hand over my heart, and I would imagine that someday they would play it for me on that Olympic podium.

I remember this past summer when my goal became real for me. I said to my coach, "Richard, I am on a mission. Every cell in my body is moving toward this goal. I am going to do everything I can to live this dream." So when it was actually happening, I was just savoring every moment.

An Olympic gold medal is not something you do on your own. There were so many times when I was ready to throw in the towel. I could not have made it through without the support of my parents, my coach, my friends, and Dr. John Moore, my chiropractor. He would sit down and help me find solutions. He even helped me with some unique chiropractic techniques. He did emotional chiropractic work called the Durlacher technique, which is based on the meridians of the body, to help me work through some mental blocks. His support made a big difference.

JD: Now, looking back on the race and your preparation, you said all the pieces came together for you. Could you tell me what the important pieces were for you?

MH: I have been practicing mental training techniques for the past three years. So the most important piece that came together for me was the mental component - just being in the right zone and having the courage to stay within myself.

Other important elements included strength, endurance, overall health, and my stroke mechanics. The underwater factors are distance per kick, rate of kick, distance per stroke, and rate of stroke, executing my turns, and managing my breathing. I needed to learn to go out fast, but do it within myself and not spend too much energy trying to get out in front. It's all about management of energy. You have to gain a feel for the pace that's best for you.

JD: Can you give an example of a specific mental strategy that worked for you?

MH: Here's one technique: I have an inner control, a key word or phrase that I use. I will say to myself: "Get on top of that, rise above it, stay in your inner control." So I'm saying, "I'm going to do this. I've made up my mind. I've made the decision to do this." That keeps me from getting overemotional and putting up a wall. I'm able to stay open and in the moment. I tend to use up all my energy leading up to the race, thinking about it too much instead of just being in the present moment.

© John Moore, D.C.

JD: Tell me about your experience in the closing ceremonies.

MH: That was my favorite memory of the Olympics. Before we went out into the stadium, all of the teams would meet in their different venues. The closing ceremonies are different from the opening ceremonies in that everybody gets mixed up together so there's no separation of team or sport. As we were walking toward the stadium, I was aware there were no divisions anymore. Everyone was just walking together. As we were walking through this long 100-yard tunnel into the stadium, I remember looking at all the athletes going through together. It didn't matter who had won or had who lost, what country you were from, or what sport you were involved in. We were all celebrating together.

Walking into the Olympic stadium in front of 100,000 people was such a powerful feeling. It was so overwhelming and inspirational. I started to cry. Everyone in the stands was waving lights back and forth. I had been through so much and won the gold medal. It was a great way to cap off that experience. There were TV cameras and media people from all over the world wanting to interview me. It was great to share my experience with them. I will remember that race for the rest of my life!

Part
II

Essential
Tools of the
Trade

Chapter
5

Mindfulness:
Conscious Breathing
and Relaxation

*Relaxation
does for the mind
what stretching
does for the body*

We are continually moving between tension and relaxation, both mentally and physically. Athletes need a certain amount of tension to be able to perform well. However, if muscles become too tight, we lose our fluidity, our sense of control. Each of us needs to find that right balance to move and stay within our comfort zone.

Haile Gebrselassie is the perfect model for relaxed running under pressure. Haile is the premier distance runner in the world and a living legend in Ethiopia. He is the latest in that country's long line of distance greats that includes Abebe Bikila, Mamo Wolde, and Miruts Yifter.

Gebrselassie, who won the 1996 and 2000 Olympic gold medals in the 10,000-meters, has an awesome combination of poise, stamina, and a devastating kick. In Sydney, while standing at the starting line of the 10,000-meter finals, most of the runners were looking tense and nervous. Haile, on the other hand, was apparently joking with someone on the sidelines. He appeared so relaxed he was actually bent over laughing while waiting for the race to start. Once the gun went off, he moved into a relaxed focus and went on to capture the Olympic gold medal.

In June, 1998, Gebrselassie recorded the 5000-meter world record of 12 minutes, 39.36 seconds in Helsinki, Finland, less than two weeks after he captured the 10,000-meter mark with a time of 26:22.75 in Hengelo, Holland. Using this relaxed stance in racing, he has set 15 world records and won four consecutive world titles in the 10,000 meters, dating back to 1993.

The most overlooked element in athletic training programs also happens to be the most crucial one for good performance - the ability to relax the mind and body. This is why champion performances look so smooth and effortless. Elite athletes consistently report that the key to smoother, faster training is to focus on being relaxed rather than trying to create more power. Trying to "muscle through" a workout can cause a lack of synchronicity in the muscle groups. For instance, the hamstrings need to be relaxed as the quads are contracting in order to move efficiently. This can be critical in the last part of a competition when fatigue sets in and the pressure mounts. Remaining loose and calm can make all the difference. It can enhance your ability to perform when it really counts.

The Meaning of Relaxation

Relaxation is an experience. It is a state of physical and mental stillness characterized by the absence of tension and anxiety. It means letting go and sometimes doing absolutely nothing with the mind and muscles. Although relaxation is one of the more natural and satisfying states that human beings can attain, the feeling of calmness must be experienced to be fully understood.

Two things happen when people discover how to relax. First, there is a physiological response. When I do biofeedback training with my clients, those who are most relaxed go into a slow, deep abdominal breathing pattern, with a decrease in heart rate. The electromyograph (EMG) shows diminished muscle tension, and the hand thermometer shows warmth, indicating more blood flow to the hands and feet.

Secondly, we find that there is a psychological response. The electroencephalograph (EEG) indicates that relaxed athletes go into an "alpha state," creating more brain waves in this very creative and healthful state of consciousness. This state enhances one's ability to concentrate and move away from anxiety and negative thoughts – a state of mind more conducive to performing well. Relaxation is also an enabling condition. When you are physically and mentally relaxed, you are empowered to accomplish feats that are not possible at other levels of consciousness.

© John Segesta – Triathlete Magazine

Why is Relaxation so Essential for Athletes?

When I work with athletes, they often have difficulty with the idea of learning relaxation. They ask: "Why should I want to relax? If I get too calm, I'll lose the excitement and won't go fast." "All those relaxation exercises are boring anyway. My mind is always racing and doesn't want to go that slow." These concerns are characteristic of the "Type A personality," which describes many athletes quite well. The primary features portray someone who is high achieving, perfectionistic, stoic, independent, and chronically tense. I often will tell an athlete client: "If you can introduce a new dimension of relaxation to your training program, you won't be taking anything away from the high achieving part of yourself. On the contrary, you will be adding to it."

Learning relaxation has many positive rewards that extend far beyond the arena of athletics. You can see gains in every part of your life. Athletes need to clear their minds and calm themselves more completely for a number of reasons:

Recharge the mind: As you learn the art of relaxation, you can quickly discharge any pressure and restore the feelings of excitement and joy about training.

Lower the risk of injury: Injury is often a result of muscle tightness. The healthiest muscles are those that are loose and relaxed.

Prepare for a competition: Calm the mind and conserve energy in the body to perform well in an important event. You need to be fully rested for maximal exertion.

Decrease stress level: Find your optimal arousal level and reduce unnecessary tension and anxiety.

Decrease fatigue: You can often exhaust yourself with the day's activities. People who are overly anxious are unconsciously contracting their muscles throughout the day, which slows down the blood flow process for rapid recovery. Periodic relaxation exercises can help you feel recharged and energetic.

Enhance quality of sleep: You reduce your internalized pressure and fall into a deep and restful sleep on the night before a competition or after traveling to a new environment.

Accelerate the natural healing process: During any given winter, chances are high that you will have a flu virus in your body. Yet your own healing system (your immune system) deals with it effectively without your awareness, as long as you are allowing yourself enough relaxation and recovery time.

Repair bone and soft tissue: Running and other weight-bearing activities are high maintenance sports. The body is constantly repairing itself. Broken bones and connective tissue strains can be healed in a shorter time with proper mental relaxation and imagery techniques.

Open and expand your consciousness: Once the mind is fully relaxed, negative thinking and self-criticism are greatly reduced. Thus, the right brain is more open to new ideas, and you can begin to work with visualization techniques in a powerful way. You can create vivid mental images of exactly what you want to happen and increase the chances of turning them into reality.

Self-Assessment for Tension and Stress

The key to successful performance in any sport is to recognize the early warning signs of rising stress levels. You need to then take immediate action to bring your stress level down, before your body is screaming at you for attention. Each person has a characteristic pattern in the response to stress. What system in your body overreacts to pressure? Do you notice any of the following reactions?

➢ Feeling fatigued
➢ Racing heart
➢ Muscle tension in jaw, neck, shoulders
➢ Rapid, shallow breathing
➢ Stomach upset or vomiting
➢ Desire to urinate
➢ Irritability
➢ Forgetting details
➢ Inability to focus or make decisions
➢ Resorting to old habits
➢ Catching colds frequently

It is important to know your individual response to stressful situations (e.g., a competition) and begin doing relaxation before the symptoms get out of hand.

Tools for Relaxation of the Mind and Body

When Wilson Kipkiter broke the world record twice in the 800 meters at the 1997 World Indoor Championships, his face looked so peaceful as he was coming around the final turn, you would think he was out for an afternoon stroll. The athletes I work with often report: "Relaxed training seems so easy it hardly feels like you're working at all."

With regular practice of breathing and relaxation techniques, you can begin to look and feel like a world-class athlete. Here are some useful strategies to take you to deeper levels of relaxation and higher levels of performance.

After practicing these techniques both at home and during training, your speed workouts will begin to feel easier. You can take your mind off the feeling of tension and fatigue, and move straight into focusing on the task at hand. You'll look forward to pressure situations as an opportunity to fine-tune your relaxation and have your body and mind perform well when it really counts.

Exercise: Breathing for Accelerated Recovery

Even without your awareness, your breathing plays a significant part in regulating your performance in sports and in life. If you change the way you breathe, you can change the way you feel. Gaining better control of your breathing allows you to take charge of your body and mind. The pattern of your breathing is quite different when you are tense, nervous, or negative than when you are calm and relaxed. Thus it is important to develop varied patterns of breathing for different purposes. Through proper breathing you can maintain the right balance between attention and relaxation. This balance is critical for precise allocation of energy when training and competing.

Relaxation training should begin with attention to your breathing. Do this exercise for 10 minutes, three times per day, to keep your stress level low and to accelerate recovery time. Begin by finding a quiet place with a comfortable chair where you will not be disturbed. Turn off your pager or phone, close your eyes, and take 10 deep breaths. Place your hand about two inches below the belly button and inhale slowly and deeply. Imagine that there is a vertical accordion running down your spine. As you breathe in, let the accordion expand outward. After a pause, begin to slowly exhale and feel the accordion collapsing back down. Pause for a few moments before taking in your next breath. Let your body feel supported by the chair. As each thought comes into your mind, just notice it. With your next exhale, let the thought go and return your focus to your breathing. Let your mind and body be at peace. Give yourself one simple, positive suggestion that you repeat three times. For example: "My mind and body are growing stronger and healthier every day."

Exercise: Stilling the Mind

Relaxing the mind is just as important as calming the muscles. Athletes need to relax the left-brain – the objective, intellectual part of the mind that is designed for thinking, analyzing, and classifying. This part of the brain is your inner critic, the part that says, "Yeah, but" or "What if." It often becomes an active resister to progress and can make it difficult to move forward with your training and other parts of your life. When you relax, the left-brain is slowed down, and the right brain becomes more active. The right brain is the creative part that is oriented toward imagery and is more accepting of new ideas.

If you have done the breathing exercise above, your mind has already begun to relax. To further calm the mind, imagine yourself training in your favorite place in nature. Bring your experience into the present tense and use all five of your senses. Hear the sound of the wind and your breathing. Feel your toe pushing off with each step. Feel your body effortlessly floating, as the time passes quickly. It seems as though you could move at this pace for a long time. While inhaling, repeat a simple word, such as "focus." As you exhale, say a word that helps you relax, like "calm." This will take your mind away from negative thoughts and will bring you into a peaceful state of consciousness. Then you can create a mental picture of your best competition experience and see it exactly the way you want it to happen.

Muscle Awareness Exercise

Try monitoring the muscle tension levels that accompany many common activities during the course of your day. Notice how you hold your wrists and shoulders while typing at the computer. How tightly are you gripping the steering wheel while driving? What muscles are you using to hold the phone; is your neck crimped? How tight are your neck and shoulders while doing your last interval of your workout? We frequently use far more muscle power than is needed to accomplish a task effectively. When athletes "muscle through" a workout, the body's natural timing, flow, and rhythm are blocked. The movement becomes jerky and uncoordinated, and fatigue can develop more quickly.

The goal in this exercise is to match the effort with the task. Top athletes are skilled in detecting subtle differences in tension levels and fine-tuning their responses. So adjust your muscle tension to whatever job you are doing. Relax the muscles that are not needed for that task.

Chapter
6

Virtual Workouts: Using Positive Imagery

Close your eyes,
open your mind,
and imagine

Meaningful achievements begin with a positive vision that we fully welcome, commit to, and strive to complete with passion. We first create a picture in the mind's eye, and we imagine what it would be like to accomplish that goal and reach our destination. Then we seek out a path - a method of traveling that will lead us to where we want to go. Finally, we step into that image and apply all our knowledge, our drive, and our power to turn the dream into reality. Creative visions and dedicated actions direct us, energize us, and inspire us to overcome obstacles to discover our performing edge.

A few years ago I had the opportunity to give a talk on mental training at Bill Rodgers and Joan Benoit Samuelson's running camp in Vermont. While out running with Joan, I asked about her mindset during her historic race in the 1985 Chicago Marathon, when she raced head-to-head with Ingrid Kristiansen, the world record holder at that time. Joan had just won her Gold Medal in the first ever women's Olympic marathon in 1984.

Joan related her experience: "That was one of the most difficult races of my life. Ingrid and I were running side-by-side on a world record pace. We were at 31 minutes at the 10K mark. I kept surging ahead, but Ingrid would always respond. I couldn't seem to shake her. I had prepared mentally for the race by using imagery. During the marathon, I would see myself running easily on my favorite ten-mile loop. Then I would picture myself on a six-mile loop, followed by another ten-mile trail run. Dividing it up in my mind that way made the race seem shorter and more enjoyable." In Chicago, Joan finally pulled away from Ingrid, winning the race in 2:21:15. She broke the American record for the marathon and ran the 2nd fastest time in history. Her U.S. record still stands today.

The utilization of mental imagery for enhanced performance is not new, as confirmed by this example. The practice of martial arts in Asia, meditation and yoga in ancient India, and hypnotherapy are other illustrations of how the mind's capacity to picture situations can be a critical part of one's athletic performance. Whereas mental training may have been viewed skeptically in the past, now imagery and other similar techniques have become an integral part of most sports programs. Serious athletes who want to engage in more complete preparation, train both their body and mind for top-level performance.

What is Mental Imagery?

Images are the mental representations of our experience. While verbal language is the most common means for communicating with the external world, imagery is a powerful means for internal communication. The visualization process can be defined as the conscious creation of mental or sensory images for the purpose of enhancing your training and your life. It is the deliberate attempt to select positive mental images to affect how your body responds to a given situation.

Just as we work out our bodies, we also need to exercise the brain. Mental training is like taking your brain to the gym. We want our bodies to have many different gears and speeds. We also need the mind to be flexible – to be able to shift into different gears depending on the task at hand. Mental imagery is a powerful tool for achieving this purpose.

By using imagery or visualization you can create, in vivid detail, a replay of one of your best performances in the past, or you can mentally rehearse an upcoming event, and you can see yourself doing it right. Imagery guides much of an athlete's experience because it is a more efficient, complete language than self-talk. Try to describe to someone how to execute the perfect freestyle swim stroke, in detail, using words. You could write a book. Now show the same stroke through a video replay of Australian Ian Thorpe (known as the Thorpedo), who dominated the swimming scene in the 2000 Olympics. You convey the exact message you want in a few seconds.

Most of us daydream and re-experience situations in our minds in a haphazard way. The fact that we can remember previous experiences in detailed fashion is why visualization works so well for athletes. Most good athletes have discovered this technique on their own and may use it occasionally to improve learning and performance. However, for maximum results, you need to control your imagery and practice it on a regular basis rather than just let thoughts pass in and out. Through imagery you can re-create your best performances in great detail, and then use that energy to help you through any situation you may encounter.

Megan Quann used the power of mental imagery to win two Olympic gold medals in Sydney. For two years prior to the 2000 Olympic Trials, Megan Quann went to bed visualizing her dream of a world record in the 100-meter breaststroke. Megan's bedroom is filled with pictures of the pools where she has had successful swims: the pool in San Antonio, Texas, where she set an American record in the 100-meter breaststroke and the pool in Sydney where she won a silver medal at the Pan-Pacific Championships.

Each night before she went to sleep, Megan would visualize herself setting a world record in the 100-meter breaststroke. She did not see herself standing on the podium. Instead, she would visualize swimming a fast race. She would lie down in bed and take some deep breaths, letting her heart rate come down to her normal resting level. Then she would reach for her stopwatch, close her eyes, and imagine herself at the Olympic pool in Sydney.

Megan describes her imagery: "They bring us out behind the starting blocks. I hear the announcer say my name and my accomplishments. Then there are three whistles. I take off my warm-ups and step up to the block. I hear, 'The 100-meter breaststroke. Take your mark.' When I hear the gun, I start the stopwatch by my bed. As I dive in, I can feel my stroke through the water. I see the tiles on the bottom of the pool. I swim to the end, touch the wall, and make my turn – 50 meters to go. I tell myself, this is it, I have to go faster. As I touch the wall, I press the button on my stopwatch. I feel my carotid artery on my neck. My heart rate has risen to 192. The watch reads 1:05 – a world record time."

Although Megan did not break the world record in Sydney, she broke the American record, and has done so several times in her event. Her personal best time of 1:07:05 makes her the second fastest woman of all time.

The Power of Imagery

Even if you are not yet accomplished in visualization techniques, it is reassuring to know that everyone has an imagination, and everyone can improve with practice. You can develop positive images and utilize the experiences and feelings that serve you best. You can take the best you have been and the best you can possibly be, incorporate that into your mind's eye, and then transform those visions into reality.

You can use visualization for virtually any goal or problem that you need to work on. Imagery can be used for reducing stress, focusing attention, energizing, problem solving, or skill learning.

I spoke with national champion Regina Jacobs two weeks before the 2000 Olympic Trials. She talked about how imagery has helped her uncover her true potential in the 1500 and 5000 meters. During visualization she incorporates all of her senses into the experience. She feels her forefoot pushing off the track, she hears her running splits, and she sees herself surging ahead of the competition. She experiences all of the elements of her race in explicit detail before executing her performance. At the 2000 Olympic Trials, Regina went on to set a new American record for the 5000 meters using mental training techniques on a regular basis. It appears generally true that athletes who are most successful have developed the psychological foundation for their performances well in advance of the actual event.

You can also use imagery for controlling emotional states, for dealing with unexpected contingencies, for centering, or for blocking distractions. Andy Palmer, Ph.D., coach, sports psychologist, and former 2:16 marathoner, tells athletes to consider using imagery as a way to deal with specific weaknesses in their workouts and races. He states: "If you tend to go out too fast in the beginning of races, try imagining that situation and mentally rehearse what you would do at the moment you know you're in trouble. You'll realize that you can be in control of the situation."

You may also use visualization to set appropriate goals, to motivate yourself, to mentally rehearse your workouts, or to manage pain during a race.

> In my interview with champion miler Marty Liquori, he noted: "I have always believed, if you want to be a champion, you will have to win every race in your mind 100 times before you win it in real life that last time."

So visualization in your mind's eye is a powerful tool. It can help improve everything you want to do. You can gain greater control over your body, mind, and emotions, and integrate them to maximize the quality of your workouts and your life. By changing the inner attitude of the mind, you can transform the outer elements of your athletic training and your life.

How does Imagery Work?

There are two primary theories that explain why visualization may have an impact on sports performance. First, images may be an efficient way of coding or representing instructions for movement. As described earlier, forming an image of a correct swim stroke provides a simpler, more complete description of the motion than is possible with words.

Secondly, when you imagine yourself performing an action, you are transmitting electrical impulses to the muscles involved in executing the action. When I do a computerized biofeedback assessment with a runner, for instance, I can place EMG electrodes on the quadriceps muscles, and we can see that those muscles are being activated as he or she visualizes running a race. During imagery, these neuromuscular impulses have the same pattern as the impulses generated when the athlete is actually running. Of course, these changes are somewhat less than those that occur when you actually perform the activity. You can't simply visualize your way to a great 10K, but the internal changes may be strengthening the neural pathways involved when these movements are performed.

Imagery Though the Senses

Now let's talk about a variety of imagery categories and see how visualization incorporates the senses. After you become familiar with the various options, you can then select a particular type of imagery that matches your own perception style. Most experts agree that for maximum effectiveness, mental images should be positive and vivid, and evoke as many senses as possible. Why should imagery be a sensory experience?

Events can be felt and remembered most vividly through the senses. When the senses are brought into an experience, it makes you pay better attention to the details of how you complete an action or skill. You can integrate your emotions and senses into the preparation for each type of action. So the goal is to fully experience everything you need to do to be successful in your performances – your training form, pacing, balance, range of motion, even your state of mind and energy level. So if you want to make a constructive change in your performance, you need to incorporate as many senses as possible into your imagery.

You may be able to see yourself bounding up a steep hill, or hear the sound of the crowd cheering you toward the finish line, or feel the speed in your legs as you surge around the curve on a track. For some athletes mental images may not be as visual but rather more kinesthetic responses. For instance, swimmers often need to have a feel for the water in order to excel in their sport.

Imagery Options

There are three primary types of imagery:

External visual imagery: You become an outside observer, as though you are watching a movie of yourself performing. This method is useful for analyzing your form or distancing yourself from pain during a race.

Internal visual imagery: You visualize from the inside of your mind and body. With this type of imagery you mentally rehearse what you actually see with your own eyes as you execute an event. It's like having a video camera on your head that records what you are seeing as you are moving.

Kinesthetic imagery: You don't see anything but you experience through your sense of touch. For instance, you feel the wind on your face or notice your arms propelling you forward as you swim or cycle.

Using the senses makes your imagery come alive. This process allows you to bring your mind, body, and spirit into your preparation. It provides a new dimension to your mental training and brings you closer to what the real situation will be like. Feeling bodily sensations as if an event were actually happening allows the body, mind, and soul to prepare more completely for an upcoming goal that you want to pursue.

You can apply the strategies above in an infinite variety of ways. Experiment with these strategies and find the ones that work best for you. Be creative and come up with your own system. Begin to notice what form your imagery takes so you can be aware of the way you experience your sport.

Here are some ideas that have dramatically improved the performances of my athlete clients. First, you can utilize what I call my "**magnet technique**." Imagine that the athlete ahead of you has a magnet on his or her back. Rather than working hard to catch up, envision the magnet drawing you toward the person effortlessly. Once you pull alongside, place the magnet on the next athlete ahead of you or at the top of the next hill.

I have used this technique many times to move ahead into the lead in triathlons and marathons. Using the mind in this way allows you to take the pressure off and have more fun with your racing. You'll find that your competition will appear less threatening because you can stay in contact with those that normally pull away in races. You'll be able to maintain a steady pace while using less energy and sustain concentration for longer periods.

> Gordon Bakoulis, 2000 Olympic marathon trials qualifier, related: "I kept an open mind while running the 2000 New York City Marathon. I found a quiet place before the start where I was able to lie down, close my eyes, and visualize the course, mile by mile. During the last, tough 10K, I imagined myself rolling up a ball of string that drew me to the finish."

Another powerful strategy I've developed is the "**funnel technique**." Using this method toward the end of a long event can make the difference between finishing strong and falling apart. During the last few minutes or miles of a long race, fatigue can easily set in. Marathoners, for example, often experience a psychological "wall" near mile 20 of the race. Try imagining you have a funnel attached to the top of your head that is gathering energy from all around you. Feel the endless reserves of strength and power filling every cell in your body. You'll begin to notice a mental and physical lift that can carry you through to the finish line.

Before I started training for my first Hawaii Ironman Triathlon, I had never attempted an event of this length. I used imagery to prepare mentally and build my confidence going into the race. Every night for six weeks prior to the race I would spend fifteen minutes visualizing the event.

On race morning, I completed the swim easily. However, the long, grueling bike ride through black lava fields took its toll. After I completed the bike ride and dismounted, I felt horrible. I had swum 2.4 miles and cycled 112 miles in 100 degrees weather, with 90 percent humidity. The sun was beating down during the hottest part of the day. I left the bike transition area and began walking the marathon course. I told myself: "26 miles, yeah right. There's no way I'm going to finish this. I might as well pack it in right now." I was doing a superb job of talking myself out of the race.

Then a woman passed me whom I had beaten in several other races. I said to myself, "Oh God, even she is passing me." She looked back and said, "Hey, Dahlkoetter, you're walking!" That's probably the best thing that could have happened. I was angry. I said to myself, "I've got to do something major here to get myself going."

I pictured in my mind a time when I felt really good on a run – the San Francisco Marathon. I visualized myself feeling powerful, relaxed, and focused. I remember the race conditions were perfect that day. The weather was cool, and I was mentally and physically prepared. My legs felt strong, and I was in "the zone." I won the race in 2:43:20, a personal record by over 20 minutes! When my consciousness shifted back to the Ironman, I found myself no longer walking. I was running well, the crowd was cheering, and I regained my energy.

After completing that mental imagery process early in the run, I realized that I could go on and possibly finish my first Ironman Triathlon. I continued to gain momentum, feeling stronger with every mile, as I moved up in the ranks. At that point, nothing could stop me.

I had begun the run in 19th place and eventually finished as 2nd woman overall – a race I will remember forever. The visualization had transformed my entire outlook and empowered me to run the race of my life.

Guidelines for Effective Imagery

Imagery is not wishful thinking or daydreaming about the great athlete you would like to be. It is a learned skill that requires effort, concentration, discipline, and regular practice to gain the maximum benefits. Here are the key principles for doing effective mental imagery:

Timing: Imagery can be used most any time - at home, or before, during, or after training and racing. In the learning phases imagery is easier to do in a quiet, non-distracting environment. Imagery is most effective when the mind is calm and the body is relaxed.

Breathing: Begin with a few minutes of deep abdominal breathing. Put one hand on your stomach about two inches below the belly button and feel your hand rise and fall with each breath. Imagine that with each inhale you are filling up a balloon inside the stomach. As you exhale, the balloon collapses back down.

Imaging: Create in your mind as vivid an image as possible of what you want to achieve in your sport. Let distracting thoughts and feelings float away as you refocus on your image.

Sensing: Bring in all five of your senses, if possible, so you can see, hear, and feel what it's like to have a great workout or race. (Taste and smell are often powerful senses for triggering memories but are often more difficult to incorporate into day-to-day imagery training.) Bring the scene into the present tense so you are totally focused on the task at hand.

Accentuating the Positive: Don't replay the mistakes. You want to remove the memory of errors. One of my athlete clients related to me: "I'm really good at negative visualization - I have so many experiences to tap into." If you see yourself doing something incorrectly, edit the film in your mind and replay it exactly as you wish it to happen. Imagine that your performance is equal to or better than your previous best.

Pacing: Mentally rehearse your training at the same rhythm and pace that you want in your performance to establish the appropriate neurological pattern within the brain.

Modeling: Use visual models and guides. Before going to sleep at night try watching a video of a superior performance. For instance, get out your recordings from the last Olympics or World

Championships. Then visualize yourself moving just as fluidly and powerfully as perhaps Tegla Loroupe or Lance Armstrong.

Turning Your Images into Reality

Each time you are energized by an experience, inspired by someone you meet, or motivated by a performance, you have the chance to anchor the memory in your mind and use that vision whenever you need it. When you revisit those positive memories on a regular basis, you can bring to mind empowering thoughts and feelings that will inspire your performances and recharge your life.

When you construct clear images of the road you want to travel and embrace those visions on a daily basis, you can start to fully utilize the power of your mind. Begin by mentally viewing your goals upon waking each morning. See yourself experiencing those actions in your mind, body, and spirit. Feel yourself doing exactly what you want to do, the way you would like to do it. Then incorporate those images during your actual day-to-day functioning.

In order to properly train the body, you must first train the mind. Inspiring images can create powerful emotions and produce superior performances. So it's best to focus on positive images and memories. At first you may not fully believe that you can perform up to the level of your visualizations. It's OK to act as if it is already happening. With practice your body will come into line with your mental images. If a negative image comes into your mind, just breathe deeply and let it go with your exhale. Then bring in a positive image with your next breath. As you practice and refine your mental training, your images will become clearer and more convincing.

Remember, mental imagery can be effective at any level of training or competition. Mental and physical training can work quite well to complement one another. The more familiar you become with the intricacies of your sport, the more effective your mental practice will become. Of course, mental imagery is not a substitute for physical training. You still have to put in the miles. But it can make all the difference in the quality and enjoyment of your training and racing. It will move you much closer to realizing your true potential.

Your Performing Edge Visualization

Find a comfortable, quiet place, close your eyes, and take 10 deep abdominal breaths, remembering to exhale fully. Recall a moment in time when you were completely engaged in what you were doing – a period when you felt optimistic and confident, not concerned about the outcome. Bring the event into the present tense and be there with all five senses. Notice everything around you – what you're doing, what you're wearing, where you are, if you are alone or with others. Become aware of how the situation evolved and what is happening at this moment. Pay close attention to your feelings, your thoughts, and your physical sensations. Do a body scan to check out how each part is working. Notice how each muscle group is feeling. Are you relaxed and yet alert? Are you energized and focused? Is your mind very active or calm? Are you enjoying yourself?

Now let an image come to mind to represent this experience. It could be a color, a shape, or a symbol – something to help you remember this wonderful moment and anchor it in your memory. Now imagine that you are placing this image in your heart. Whenever you want to re-experience these feelings (for instance, in your next workout or competition), you can simply recall your symbol, and you can recapture all that power, confidence, and focus any time you need it.

After you complete your session, open your eyes and write down your impressions of the experience. You can write in prose or in single words or phrases – note anything that comes to mind. If you choose, you can draw your images. There is no right or wrong to your imagery. Just accept whatever you experience, without judgment, and draw the meaningful connections.

Chapter
7

Language for Success:
Creative
Affirmations

*Performance is
90% perception
and
10% reality*

Words can have tremendous power over our minds and, subsequently, our athletic performance. It has been said: Performance is 90% perception and 10% reality. Each of us is constantly engaging in our own internal thought processing. We talk to ourselves and interpret each situation based on our perception of what is going on around us. If this self-talk is an accurate representation of reality, then we function quite well. If our thoughts are irrational or exaggerated, then we may become anxious or emotional, and performance is likely to decline.

Reconstructing Your Thoughts

Thoughts and attitudes are cognitive in nature. Our perception and thoughts often lead to an emotional response. These thoughts and emotions then provide the direction and control over our actions. Thus it is crucial to become aware of what thoughts and self-statements you are using prior to training or racing.

Self-talk can provide a sense of control if you learn to become aware of self-statements and direct them in a positive manner. You can, through self-talk, evaluate a potentially negative situation as much less threatening once you have a sense of control over your thought processes. How you interpret what is happening and the kinds of labels you place on each situation determine how you are affected emotionally.

Defining Affirmations

One powerful way to structure our thoughts and transform our goals into results is through the use of affirmations. An affirmation is a strong, positive self-statement, spoken in the present tense, about a goal that has the potential for being realized. It is a pre-planned statement of an aspiration, presented to the mind as if it has already been achieved. You present it to the mind in the present rather than the future tense. Although intellectually you know your goal is in the future, successful mental programming dictates that it be stated in the present tense as an already realized fact.

Affirmations are a powerful way to cancel or correct old negative thoughts or ideas. Negative thoughts are carried in our mental computers and are the source of self-limitation, fear, inhibition, and frustration for all of us. In contrast, self-image, health, physical abilities, relationships, and competition can all be affected positively by the repetition of an affirmation.

A positive affirmation creates an attitude or posture in life that says: "I can do this!" It is a conscious, carefully worded positive statement that guides our behaviors in a constructive way. It empowers us to replace old pessimistic scripts with new creative phrases to help us realize our dreams. Words are effective tools for transforming our perception of daily events.

The mind and body are so well connected that the body often does not know whether a phrase or image is real, dreamed, or imagined. So when your mind creates an image of success, your central nervous system and whole body will process that image as if it were real. Most of the time our actions are reflections of our mental pictures. These pictures are placed in our mind most often by words. So choosing the right words can make or break a performance.

I often use affirmations with my athlete clients to assist them in reconstructing their thoughts. If athletes find themselves saying: "I've never been able to beat this person before in a race," they are preparing themselves to lose again in this situation. I would help them to say something like: "I know I am capable of beating this person. All I have to do is take it one mile at a time. I have to focus on what is happening and what is about to happen. I can then control my own performance. I have worked hard, and I am well prepared for this competition."

How are Affirmations Used?

Whenever you want to maximize your chances of getting the results you want, affirmations are one of the fastest ways to arrive there. If you want to create real changes in the way you train and race, use affirmations to:

- Improve concentration
- Relax and sleep well
- Build self-confidence
- Accelerate learning of athletic skills
- Deal with fear and negativity
- Heal quickly from injuries
- Increase endurance and strength
- Train faster and more efficiently

Guidelines for Using Affirmations

The subconscious mind is literal or factual in nature, just like the hard drive of a computer. It receives information exactly the way you present it. Thus, in using affirmations it's best not to use statements that are negative (e.g., "I hope I don't bonk in this race"). If I say: "Don't think of pink elephants," what's the first thing that pops into your mind? You end up drilling into your mind the very thing you're trying to avoid doing. Thus, affirmations need to be presented in a specific way to optimize their effectiveness.

I was recently working with a bicycle racer, Jill, who had a fear of riding in large groups. She had fallen down several times while riding in a close pack and would get anxious whenever she got too close to other riders. The problem intensified whenever she was riding in a road race, having to make sharp turns in close quarters. I asked Jill, what are you saying to yourself while you're riding? She answered, "I repeat to myself over and over: I hope I don't crash, I hope I don't crash." Can you guess what happened after that? She was continually programming her mind and body to anticipate crashing. Consequently, she was bracing herself, holding her arms and shoulders so tightly that she could not handle the bike effectively. I then taught her to turn her goals into positive self-statements: "I am riding the bike smoothly and easily." "I am growing more relaxed with each mile." That was a turning point for Jill's cycling career. For the first time, she could really enjoy riding.

Principles to Follow in Constructing Affirmations

Use the present tense: Act as if it's already happening. If you have a race coming up, avoid using the future tense because the mind will see it as if it were still in the future. Instead of saying, "I will be strong and fast," say, "I am strong and fast." Or you can say, "I am becoming stronger and faster every day."

Employ a positive outlook: When you use negative words, they may be taken in by the brain without your awareness. Affirm what you do want to happen rather than what you don't want to occur. Rather than saying, "I won't tighten up in races," say "I remain relaxed and focused at all times."

Use self-image statements: Whenever possible, construct affirmations beginning with "I" or "I am..." or "I enjoy...."

Use specific, brief phrases: Make each phrase a short, clear statement of your feelings, so that you can remember the phrase, and the mind can then take it in more easily.

Make them permanent: Use the words "I always...."

Use mood words: Include words that suggest strong, positive emotion: "I always get excited and enthusiastic at races."

Anticipate success: When creating your affirmations, don't let your critical side limit the type of phrases you create. Use whatever thoughts seem to work for you.

Use cards or post-its: Write each affirmation on an individual index card or post-it, and place them where you can view them regularly - by your desk, refrigerator, or at a night stand.

Now that we've learned the basic guidelines for using affirmations, we can discuss specific ways to use positive self-talk for any problem you want to address.

We often find that our minds are flooded with distorted thoughts that we accept as true (e.g., "Just face it, I'm a slug, I'll never get any faster"). You may have heard the phrase "stinkin' thinkin'." This expression most accurately describes the negative thought pattern that people tend to fall into when they are lacking self-confidence. When you're not aware of what is happening in your mind, this destructive pattern can snowball and become bigger than life. If you can catch yourself in the early stages, before your thinking gets out of control, you can change the way you talk to yourself and perhaps explore a new path.

You need to keep experimenting with new ways of thinking until you can say, this one is right for me. Next time you're upset, listen to the words you use with yourself. Notice if they are reinforcing old, worn out ways of thinking or encouraging a fresh outlook. Try to choose words that invite constructive changes.

Moving From Negative to Affirmative

Let's now take time to explore some of your negative thought traps. What are the bad thought habits that you consistently use to interpret daily events in a way that brings you down? Even the most rational person on earth functions at some distance from reality. The cognitive distortions we use often have no basis in reality. Yet as long as we ruminate about them, they hold power over us. Below I have listed some common negative self-statements that come from my athlete clients. Then I provide a possible constructive counter-statement that you might substitute in your mind.

Change: "I never train well in bad weather."
   To: "I perform well under any conditions." "I am extremely flexible and adjustable." "I handle adversity quite well."
Change: "I hate climbing hills."
   To: "Hills are my friends." "These hills are fatigue-proofing my legs." "I can float up this hill like a gazelle."
Change: "I'm too fat and too slow."
   To: "My legs are getting stronger and faster everyday." "I float and glide along the trails."

Change: "I get distracted so easily."
    To: "I can concentrate fully and stay in the moment." "I am able to re-focus quickly." "I'm only thinking about what I need to do at this time."

Notice what areas of training you are struggling with and create your own positive counter-statements to move closer to your goals.

Using Thoughts as a Form of Energy

Positive self-statements can be programmed deeply into your mind if you repeat them several times while in a relaxed state. You might also want to combine them with a visualization process so you picture yourself achieving your goal as you reinforce it verbally with affirmations. You can also say them to yourself as you go about the day. Try saying them as you look into the mirror upon first rising in the morning and before retiring. Commuting to and from work is a great time to recite affirmations, or while walking, or waiting in line at the grocery store.

One powerful way to take in positive information is to hear it from your own voice: Record a tape on which you give instructions to take ten deep breaths, then repeat each of your affirmations slowly three times. You can also read any quotations from other writers that you find particularly inspirational. Then play the tape before bedtime. Your subconscious mind will work with this information during sleep. Also, type up your affirmations on cards and place them in strategic places around the house and work.

Notice the type of language you use in your conversations with people. As you talk about, say, your upcoming marathon, do you characterize it as a long, arduous, painful task? Or do you describe it as an exciting endurance adventure. Try incorporating helpful affirmations into your conversations with people and notice how they tend to respond with positive statements. You can also ask others to give you affirmations (e.g., remind you that you are a capable, energetic athlete).

Now, try mentally programming your goals and make them come alive by turning them into positive self-statements. Take each one of your goals and phrase it as an affirmation. Here is an example:

Your Goal: To become stronger and faster in your upcoming event.
Affirmation: "My body and mind are growing stronger and healthier each moment." "Every day I am moving closer to my goal."

Finally, you can notice how your affirmations are modeled in the environment. If, for instance, you want to run lightly, with soft, quiet feet, observe how your cat moves around the room. Then give yourself permission to run gracefully just like that animal.

A precautionary note needs to be provided at this point. Affirmations should not be used alone to cover up a deep emotional conflict. They are best employed in conjunction with a variety of other methods. If you are feeling particularly sad or depressed, honor your feelings and take them as warning signs that something inside needs to be addressed. First, take immediate steps to explore your mental state and deal directly with the problem. You could perhaps talk to a friend, see a sports psychologist, or write out your thoughts in a journal. Once you are feeling better, then use affirmations to reinforce a foundation of inner strength that can allow you to move forward.

Remember, affirmations are essential tools to help you focus on personal strengths. Every great performance is given by an athlete who has conditioned the mind to see the possibility of achieving that performance.

Affirmations for Competition

Racing is one area where plenty of negative thinking occurs and where affirmations can be particularly effective. If you have trouble with the competitive environment, think of the positive benefits of racing and write them down as affirmations:

➢ I am well prepared, rested, and ready for this event.
➢ Racing gives me a chance to celebrate my fitness.
➢ I gain energy from other athletes in the race.
➢ We can all help each other do our best in this race.
➢ In a race I can be towed along to a new personal record.
➢ I am a strong, capable athlete.
➢ I love racing; I am totally focused.

Try creating your own affirmations and repeating each of them to yourself 3-5 times on a daily basis. Notice how your attitude begins to improve over time during training and racing.

Chapter
8

Visionary Goals:
Tools for
Motivation

*Goals provide
direction
to your
training
and your life*

The resources of the human body and mind are enormous, often beyond our comprehension. We can tap into these hidden resources by setting goals for ourselves and passionately pursuing them. Goals are essential for making consistent progress in any training program. They provide direction, reminding us where we are going and how we plan to get there. Goals give shape to our dreams and aspirations. They help us to set priorities and work within a time frame. Once we have our goals, the mind can focus on achieving them despite any obstacles that might arise.

Before the start of the 1996 Olympic games in Atlanta, Michael Johnson, wearing his sparkling golden track shoes, said in an interview: "I like doing things that have not been done before. This year I want to win both the 400-meters and the 200-meters in the Olympics. When I set a goal for myself, and I do that every year, that is all I need to keep myself motivated." Michael Johnson's achievement of that goal was a historic moment in track and field, smashing his own one-month-old world record in the 200-meters, with an astounding 19:32. Passion, desire, and consistency in following his training plan allowed Michael Johnson to turn his goals into reality.

Going into the 2000 Olympic Trials, Michael Johnson set even higher goals. In his interview before the 400-meter final, he said: "In the Sydney Olympics, everyone is pulling out all the stops. When you get to the Olympic games, it doesn't matter what you did last year or even last week. Everybody wants to win today, and that's all that counts. I have got more to lose here than there is to gain. I hate to lose, but I'm not afraid of losing. I like to set goals and take chances. The safe way is not an option for me." Michael went on to accomplish his goal and win the gold medal once again in the 400-meters.

Goals: The Mechanism for Motivation

Regardless of performance level, athletes are always looking for ways to motivate themselves, meet new challenges, rise above adversity, and overcome setbacks. Goal setting is the primary mechanism for building motivation and commitment to personal excellence. It gives us a starting point for action, a purpose for our efforts, and a way to direct our energy effectively over time.

Eileen Portz-Shovlin, senior editor of *Runner's World Magazine*, knows about the value of goals. When I asked her how she stays motivated to run, she told me: "The way I maintain my enthusiasm is to set goals and create variety in my training. Each day I try to think of a specific purpose for my workout. There are different paces I can run, on a variety of courses and terrains. I can get a vigorous workout on some runs, while others are just for relaxation. My goal is to be creative with my training; that way I don't slip into a rut."

When I gave a sports psychology talk at the San Francisco Marathon, I asked the runners (who were set to run 26.2 miles the next day), "How many of you have goals?" Most people raised their hands. Then I asked: "How many of you have your goals written down?" Fewer hands went up. Then I asked: "How many of you have your written goals with you right now?" Only a couple of hands crept up. Establishing objectives in written form and keeping them close at hand are important indicators of one's level of commitment.

> At the 2000 Olympic track and field trials, Maurice Green established a specific goal going into the 100-meter finals. Right before the race, he wrote on a small piece of paper the time he wanted to run: "9.76." He placed that paper in the heel of his track shoe and took off down the straightway. Carrying his written goal with him, he won the Olympic Trials in an excellent time and went on to win the Olympic gold medal in Sydney.

My work with elite athletes, as well as my experience as a top-level runner and triathlete, has helped me to realize the differences between those who reach their objectives and those who fall short. It is their ability to set goals and their level of determination. Those who succeed choose their priorities carefully. They consider time constraints and other responsibilities, such as family and work, when setting goals. They set up a plan that is in line with how much time and effort they have available. Those who fall short are often unrealistic about their goals and the amount of time they can devote to them. To avoid this pitfall, evaluate the importance of reaching your goals, how much time you have to pursue them, and what you are willing to give up to meet your objectives.

Research in the area of goal setting during the 1980's and 1990's has generated several conclusions about the positive effects of goal setting. Goal setting gives our actions direction, moves us toward an objective, helps us maintain momentum, and builds motivation. Goals can be viewed as the regulators of our motivation. They can enhance our sense of direction and move us closer to our true potential.

Creating Goals That Work For You

The way you approach your goals can have a powerful effect on the outcome. Several factors make goal setting more effective. They include the types of goals set, the way they are measured, and how they are evaluated. Here are some principles to keep in mind when establishing your program:

Set challenging yet realistic goals: Be honest in evaluating your abilities as an athlete; your talents may exceed what you imagine them to be. Be realistic about the amount of time and energy you can put into your program. An unrealistic goal will only lead to frustration and disappointment. On the other hand, a goal that is too easy and immediately obtainable provides no sense of accomplishment. For example, if you want to break 40 minutes in the 10k, but your best time to date is 47 minutes, your goal is too bold. Yet cutting your time by only 10 seconds would leave little feeling of progress. Instead, try to improve your time by 30 seconds. If you reach that mark, try for another 30 seconds, and so on.

Create measurable goals: Your goals should be specific rather than general. They should provide a framework for evaluating your progress and adjusting your goals if necessary. If your coach says: "I want you to hustle more in your next workout," how will you determine when this goal has been met? Challenge yourself with a specific goal or series of goals. If your goal is to swim 4 x 100 meters freestyle, leaving on 2:15, with every other length hard, you'll know exactly where you stand. You can reward yourself for the progress made or readjust your times if the goal is unrealistic.

Make your goal public: Research has shown that those who make their goals public in some way perform significantly better than those who keep their goals to themselves. Telling a trusted friend or relative about your specific goal (e.g., to complete your upcoming sprint triathlon in under four hours) can be quite effective. You can then create a support system and have someone with whom to share your efforts and receive valuable feedback.

Set both long-term and short-term goals: Successful athletes devise short-term goals that bring them closer to their final goals. Many athletes make the mistake of skipping short-term goals. I have clients who come into my office with a long-term goal of running a sub-three-hour marathon (7-minute pace per mile), even though they have never run that pace in a 10K race. My suggestion in a case like that is to set a short-term goal of running a 10K at a 7-minute pace. Then, with proper strength and endurance training, it's reasonable to set a long-term goal of running a marathon at a pace 30 seconds per mile slower three to four months later.

Focus on aspects within your control: Olympic athletes often make comments like: "I'm going for the gold; anything less than that will be a failure." Predicting that you will win a race implies that you have control over the performance of other athletes. That's a built-in formula for frustration and failure. Instead, direct your energies toward aspects of your training and competition that are potentially within your control: your schedule, plan, diet, warm-up, form, mental focus, and effort level. Avoid focusing on elements that are beyond your control such as placing, winning, the weather, and other competitors. Direct your energy toward yourself and your own performance.

© Krysia Pohl

Now that we've established the important elements of setting goals, let's look at some ways to help ensure that these goals lead to the desired results. Setting a goal is the first step; achieving it requires commitment and passion. You have to want to be the best athlete you can be, even when obstacles arise. Here is a list of strategies for moving beyond the mental and physical barriers toward your destination.

Guidelines for Goal Realization

Establish personal goals: Make sure you set goals that matter to you. You need to believe in them, and then commit yourself to following a daily regimen that will allow you to achieve your objective.

Put your goals in writing: Carry them with you; type them into your computer; post them in a prominent place where you can see them every day.

Choose a goal partner: Find someone of equal ability to train with who can share your goal.

Establish a time frame: Build in target dates for competitions or timed workouts on your own to measure your progress.

Build flexibility into your goals: Allow for changes if they become necessary. If a muscle strain or injury occurs, your body is telling you to back off and reassess your goals.

Evaluate effort as well as performance: After a competition, assess your athletic form and level of concentration as well as your time, score, and place.

Visualize your goal: Clearly see yourself doing what it takes to reach your goal; imagine how it would feel to actually achieve it.

Create positive affirmations for your goal: Make statements to yourself that create the focus and confidence you need to accomplish your objective (e.g., "My body and mind are growing stronger and healthier every day.")

Evaluate your plan and reinforce your progress: Assess your training program daily and reward yourself regularly for making progress toward your goals (e.g., put gold stars in your log book for achieving personal records in your workouts).

Build enjoyment into your goal: Rather than becoming fixated on the outcome, learn to enjoy the process of getting there, the gratification of becoming more fit every day.

Claudia Piepenburg competed in the 1988 Olympic Marathon Trials and is editor of *Peak Running Performance Magazine*. She talks about the importance of thinking long-term, and says: "You must be patient. Set goals for yourself six months to a year down the road, not two or three months from now."

The most important step in any major accomplishment is setting a specific goal. So set goals, commit yourself to them, and work your hardest to achieve them. You will reach some goals and miss others, but at least you will have the satisfaction of knowing where you are going. The goal-setting process for your training program can then be easily applied to enhance every other aspect of your life. You may well find that you enjoy the journey even more than reaching the final destination.

If you have a goal in life that takes a lot of energy, that requires a lot of work, that incurs a great deal of interest, and that is a challenge to you, you will tend to look forward to waking up and seeing what the new day brings. An intelligent plan is the first step toward success. Planning is the open road to your destination.

Breathing Awareness

Before doing the affirmations below, begin to relax with this simple breathing exercise:

1) Lie down on the floor or couch with your arms at your sides and your palms up. Keep your legs straight and slightly apart with your toes pointed outwards and your eyes closed.

2) Scan your body for stress or tension, especially the neck, shoulders, throat, chest, and stomach.

3) Become aware of your breathing by placing one hand on your chest and one hand on your abdomen. Notice which area moves more as you breathe. If the majority of movement is in your chest, then you are probably not making full use of the lower part of your lungs. Taking short, shallow breaths only in the upper chest area is usually a sign of nervousness or anxiety.

4) Now work on your abdominal breathing. Place one hand on your lower stomach just below the navel to check your breathing. Take full, deep breaths, allowing the air to move all the way down into your lower lungs. Notice how your abdomen rises with each breath in and falls with each breath out.

5) Try breathing through your nose and out through your mouth.

6) Notice if your chest is moving in synchronicity with your abdomen. Let your chest follow the movement of your abdomen.

Affirmations for Your Goals

➢ "My goals are challenging, yet realistic."
➢ "I trust that I have what it takes to achieve my objectives."
➢ "I am flexible in my goals; I adjust them as necessary."
➢ "Each day I visualize myself taking steps to meet my goals."
➢ "I believe in my ability to achieve my goal."
➢ "Every cell in my body is moving toward this goal."
➢ "I am doing everything possible to live my dream."

Part
III

The Optimal
Performance
Mindset

Chapter
9

Building Your Confidence
and
Self Image

*Go confidently
in the
direction
of your dreams*

Marty Liquori was ranked the number one miler in the world in 1971, and now he produces ESPN's "Running and Racing" program. During an interview, I asked Marty to tell me about a race experience that was central in building his self-confidence. He explained: "The breakthrough race for me had to be the King Games in 1971 when I ran against Jim Ryan. I was 20 years old at the time. In '68 Ryan had beaten me, and he had been the top miler for many years. He retired, but then returned to racing.

"Ryan was a formidable problem for me. He was the world record holder who had not been beaten by an American for many years. It seemed like he was invincible. But one day I realized that he was not any superhuman being. I began to see him as just another person out there. I recognized that he puts on his pants one leg at a time just like everybody else. And once you come to understand that, a whole world opens up for you.

"That realization enhanced my confidence in my ability to defeat him. I was committed to doing whatever it took to win. One hour before the King Games race I went into a zone. I would not talk to people; I focused intently. People thought I was a jerk since I had just talked to them two hours before. But I needed that time to concentrate, and it paid off. I made the decision I would not let Ryan get in front of me. Building on that confidence going into the race, I responded every time Ryan tried to pass, and I ended up with the victory."

Confidence, positive self-image, and optimism are all key factors in determining how you view an athletic challenge and transform it into a powerful performance. Developing a realistic, healthy self-image is the foundation for success in sports. Once you know yourself well and are confident in your abilities, you're well on your way to realizing your goals in any sport. Self-confidence gives you the ability to create and sustain an optimal performance state regardless of the external conditions.

> Fortunately, confidence, discipline, courage, and commitment are all part of a constellation of mental skills that are learned and not inherited. Consequently, with continued practice and determination, they can become part of your skill set as well.

> Mary Ellen Clark, one of America's top divers, has enjoyed a 26-year career in her sport. Before she left her hometown to compete in the 1996 Summer Olympics in Atlanta, her friends surprised her with a "good luck" party. They gave her a gym bag full of presents to boost her confidence going into the competition. One of the gifts she received was a Wheaties box with a mirror attached to the front. She explained: "I saw that Mary Lou Retton had gotten her picture on that cereal box and I thought, 'Wouldn't that be the coolest thing, to have that happen to me?' So my friends gave me this Wheaties box with a big mirror on the front. This way, no matter what happens in the Olympics, I'm on the Wheaties box."

Sometimes it takes this type of tactic to remind us of our self worth. Champions have a strong, unwavering belief in themselves and their ability to perform well. Their confidence is so deep it is almost indestructible, unaffected by outside influences. Supremely self-confident athletes are resilient to setbacks, can shrug off pressure, and are not easily intimidated. Six-time Hawaii Ironman Champion Mark Allen has a presence about him - an extraordinary self-assurance that can, at times, appear intimidating to others. His internal belief in himself is apparent in his outward appearance.

Self-image: The Foundation of Successful Performance

Self-esteem and positive self-image are essential for performing well in any sport. One of the main factors differentiating humans from other animals is the awareness of self. We have the ability to form an identity and then attach a value to it. We define ourselves by certain standards and then we decide if we like ourselves. The struggle that often occurs comes from the human capacity for self-judgment. If you reject or criticize yourself for doing poorly in a race, you'll find yourself avoiding anything that might bring on the pain of further self-rejection. So you take fewer risks in training and racing, as well as in social and professional situations. In short, you limit your ability to realize your full potential.

The good news is that you can learn to stop making these judgments and direct your energies toward building a more constructive self-image. You can change how you feel about yourself. You can learn to recognize your positive qualities and acquire an attitude of acceptance toward yourself and others. Once those perceptions change, you will see improvements in your training and in every part of your life with a gradually expanding sense of inner freedom.

Self-Image Assessment

Before you begin to work on your self-image, it's important to do an honest self-inquiry to determine your strengths and weaknesses. Don't be afraid to put yourself under a microscope. You need to generate an objective picture of the real you - the way you see yourself and your current athletic performance. Look in the mirror and ask yourself, "Exactly what do I see?" You can fool others, but you should not be able to fool yourself. You must recognize your weaknesses and negative qualities before you can even think about correcting them.

1) Create a list of strengths and assets: List your physical attributes, your accomplishments in all areas, your character strengths, and the qualities you appreciate in yourself (e.g., "I have a strong drive to perform well; I am an easy person to get along with; I have strong character; and I am well-rounded").

2) Identify your weaknesses: Think of the qualities that you would like to improve. Take care to use only accurate, non-judgmental descriptions. Think about your sports performance as well as general personality characteristics (e.g., "I lose my focus halfway to the finish line").

3) Consider negative attitudes that hinder performance: Do you frequently use any of the following self-statements that undermine your self-image and keep you from doing your best?
Self-condemnation:
"I tend to have bad luck; something always goes wrong."
"I do well in training but not in races."
"I keep making the same mistakes in my training."
Poor self-confidence:
"My competition is so much better than I am."
"I'm too old, too slow, too short, too overweight, etc."
"I'm not prepared for this race."
Fear:
"I'm afraid I'm never going to get any better."
"When the pressure is on, I know I'll screw up."
"I'm afraid I'll make stupid mistakes."

Perfectionism:
"I fear I won't live up to the high standards I've set for myself."
"I'm never content with my performance."
Lack of competitive spirit:
"I can never get psyched up for a race."
"I don't have a killer instinct."
"I give up too easily during critical points in the race."
"I wimp out in the important competitions."
Anger and blame:
"I get so angry at myself that I can't focus on what I have to do."
"I get mad at things I can't control: the weather, my competition."
Racing mind:
" I try to recall everything I've learned but it's all jumbled in my mind."
"When I get to a race, I can't relax; I'm thinking of 10 things at once."

4) Do a Self-evaluation rating:

Rate yourself from 1-10 (definite no = 1 to definite yes = 10) on the following questions:
Confidence:
Do you have a high expectation that you will do your best in training and racing?
Do you get excited about the idea of accepting a challenge?
Do you have feelings of strength and being in control?
Do you like yourself?
Are you satisfied with your current level of sports performance?
Self-esteem Issues:
Are you a perfectionist?
Do you have extreme vulnerability to criticism?
Are you nonassertive?

There are no right or wrong answers to these questions and no bottom line score to worry about. Once you've completed your self-evaluation, you then have a solid base of information from which to work on your confidence and self-esteem.

If you can identify with a number of the issues above, it stands to reason that your performance may be suffering. It may seem like a difficult task to overcome these barriers, but the reconditioning process for building your self-confidence is simple and direct. Just like your physical training, mental conditioning takes practice and patience.

Change Your Weakness Into Power

If you are content with a mediocre performance, you will never challenge yourself to fully reach your potential in a competition. If you really want to improve your training and build confidence, you need to go out of your way to address and correct your weaknesses. Many athletes fail in their workouts because they are unable to overcome a singular personal deficiency. It's easy for us to adopt a negative attitude toward our weaknesses. We can justify them by saying that we were born with this particular problem, or we have since acquired it and there is nothing we can do about it. Or we can defend a weakness, and in the process we may start to structure our lives around it. We make the weakness the center of our thinking instead of facing the issue head on and conquering it.

> Leontien Zijlaard, a cyclist from the Netherlands, won two gold medals in the 2000 Olympics in Sydney. Her medals signified a triumph over adversity and a battle within herself. The problem began in 1992 when she was on top of her sport. A one-dimensional emphasis on cycling had led to an eating disorder. She related, "I was too heavy to climb hills very well; then it started. I would eat nothing at the dinner table and then my family would be fighting with me. My father and mother would say, 'You have a problem.' I would say, 'You're crazy, I am the world champion.'
>
> "My muscles were empty. I would spend a lot of time in front of the mirror. I would say, 'I am fat here; I have to lose weight there.' There was definitely depression going on. It wasn't about cycling; it was about my life. Then I spent three years away from the sport, fluctuating between 98 lbs. and 175 lbs." Zijlaard's husband helped her to see something on the inside that enabled her to feel really good about the outside. She noted: "It's very difficult to find the middle ground. For me, it's always been black and white. I needed to look inside myself and face the problem. Now I try to do more things in the middle. My weakness became my strength and I was able to win gold in the Olympics."

So to build confidence, you must first understand your problem areas, as you have done in the Self-Image Assessment. Then go to work. Make the weakest link in your chain strong and you can't help but improve. The best athletes in the world are those who actively work to overcome their weaknesses. It's fun to practice your

© Graham Watson

strengths because those are the areas in which you excel and can easily get positive feedback. But the way to truly improve is to test yourself, notice where you are making mistakes, face them, and turn them around.

For instance, the next time you do a race and a competitor surges ahead of you, see if you can stay with him or her and use that athlete's energy to pull you along to a personal best. If you cannot meet the challenge, you'll know it's time to go back to the pool or the track and work on the ability to change paces and recover quickly within the workout.

When a race is on the line, there is no substitute for skill. If you have addressed your weaknesses, you won't be vulnerable. You'll be fully prepared, confident, and ready to encounter anything the competition might give you.

Enhancing Your Confidence and Self-Image

Now that you've gained information about your confidence level, you can begin to work on your self-image using some of the techniques outlined below. Try out each one and choose the strategies that seem to fit best for you.

Separate who you are from what you have achieved: Athletes frequently use their stopwatch, their scores, or their performances to define their self-worth. They may say: "I need to run a sub-40 minute 10K in order to feel OK about myself." A disappointing race performance does not indicate that you are a poor athlete, nor is it a commentary on your real potential. You need to begin with a firm foundation, a secure sense of self. Consciously lighten up on harsh self-judgments. Come to accept yourself as a valuable person regardless of the outcome.

Awareness of Subtle, Degrading Self-Statements: Work to diminish the intensity of your negative self-attacks while nourishing more healthy self-talk. You may never entirely turn off the inner voice that says: "You really screwed up that workout; you're stupid". However, you can tone down its volume and significance. When someone gives you a compliment, rather than dismissing it, take it in and let it enhance your self-esteem.

Choose a Positive Quality You Want to Develop: Let's say you want to train more efficiently, with a sense of confidence, lightness, and power. Select another athlete who possesses these qualities and visualize that person's style during your workout. Imagine that you are that athlete, floating effortlessly, with endless amounts of energy and self-assuredness.

> Marion Jones, winner of five track and field medals at the 2000 Olympics in Sydney, visualized other top athletes to give her inspiration. In may interview with her, she said, "I hope to be considered one of the best athletes ever. Whenever I watch the Evelyn Ashfords and the Jackie Joyner Kersees, I see the sparkle in their eyes. I don't know what they're feeling, but whatever it is, I know I want some of that."

Building confidence is critical to good performance, and many other attributes follow in its wake. Self-confident athletes are also optimistic, motivated, focused, and unafraid to take risks. They move toward challenges with inner strength and courage and find personal rewards in each endeavor, regardless of the outcome. As your self-image becomes more positive, the degree of excellence will correspondingly rise in all areas of your life.

Positive Affirmations for Confidence
Repetition of Strengths: Take your list of personal strengths from your evaluation and build positive affirmations around each one. Create simple positive phrases that you can say to yourself silently or aloud, to reinforce your positive qualities. Here are some examples:

➢ I strive to be positive and enthusiastic, no matter what happens.
➢ I feel a sense of power, confidence, and inner strength when I compete.
➢ I thoroughly enjoy myself as I train and race.
➢ I am consistently working to address my weaknesses.
➢ I am a smooth, efficient athlete; I am improving rapidly.
➢ I simply perform; the results will take care of themselves.
➢ I sense that my body and mind are growing stronger and healthier every day.
➢ I accept my mistakes as simply feedback; they are a necessary part of learning anything well.
➢ I focus on doing the very best I can at every moment.
➢ I am willing to do whatever it takes to meet my goal.
➢ I believe in myself; I radiate an inner confidence.

Chapter
10

Concentration: Focusing Your Energies

Mental discipline creates performance

A thletes invariably want to improve their ability to concentrate. Mentally tough competitors can maintain concentration close to 100 percent of the time they are training and racing. A great athlete going into action is the picture of perfect concentration. No one needs to be convinced of its importance. Maintaining focus is the key to success in sports and in most activities in life, but we rarely practice it in a systematic way.

If you watch Olympic Gold Medalist Joan Benoit Samuelson at the starting line of a marathon, you can see an intense and thoughtful face - the look of someone mentally preparing for a peak performance. Just before the gun goes off, there is a moment of solid, uninterrupted concentration. She focuses her attention on a single idea for a given period of time and prepares to apply her full mental energy throughout the race. Once the race begins, Joan is the picture of unwavering attention on the task at hand, a metronome of even pacing and smooth striding. It is not until she approaches the finish line that she shows her emotions and celebrates her achievement.

Are You Concentrating or Contemplating?

Building concentration means developing the ability to reduce extraneous thoughts and attention to non-relevant cues that distract you when you compete and train. Concentration is not contemplating - that's an intellectual process in which you think about the past and future. Contemplating involves an intellectual understanding of how something could have happened, or what would have happened if.... You take apart the pieces and examine them.

During concentration, the past and future fade away; you stay with the present. You are not concerned about the results because you are only aware of one thing (e.g., your breathing or the athlete in front of you, etc.). When you concentrate, you are being fascinated by something. For example, you may become so absorbed in a movie that you're oblivious to the person sitting next to you getting up and leaving. (Obviously they weren't as absorbed as you!)

Figure and Ground

Concentration is a natural function of the brain. We tend to arrange the stimuli in our environment into patterns (Gestalts) and pay attention to one object or event at a time. We divide our visual field into figure and ground. What do you make the figure (the important object of focus), and what do you make the ground (the backdrop)? Are the spectators too far in the forefront; or does the pain in your stomach capture too much of your attention? Distractions frequently become too prominent in our minds, and the important task at hand often fades into the background.

The primary difference between concentrating and simply attending to something is that concentration is deliberate and controlled - it doesn't waver. The mind is a gypsy, always moving and shifting. It can sometimes prevent us from fully committing our energies to one endeavor. We often miss obvious chances to do well in an activity due to lack of concentration. However, you can learn techniques to reduce distractions and expand the length of time you can focus on a single activity.

Focusing at the Right Moment

Now let's discuss how you can use concentration in the sports arena. Competitions provide a myriad of opportunities for you to execute your best performance. All you have to do is be aware of them. You need to have your focus in the right place when the action is happening.

Let's say you are in a challenging pack of five people, halfway through a race, digging deep for every ounce of energy, as you are hanging on to their heels. Gradually, the leaders begin to pull away by two feet. The move is happening so slowly that you hardly notice the pace is accelerating. You are becoming more fatigued in the final stages of the race and "zoning out" - losing your focus. The pack is starting to leave you behind. This is a critical point in the race where you need to be mentally alert and make a conscious decision to stay with them. You could intensify your focus (e.g., say to yourself: "This is my free ride to the finish line") and use their energy to pull you to a new personal record, or you could let this opportunity slip through your fingers as you lose contact with the pack. You see the other athletes moving on as you let your feelings of fatigue take over, and you trudge in to finish in a mediocre time. The key is in your ability to concentrate during the crucial points of the race and draw on all the positive energy that is around you.

Focusing under Pressure

There are certain points during training or competing when you need to dig down deep and direct all of your attention to what's happening right in front of you. Other times you can relax and let your body do what you've trained it to do, without much coaxing.

What about the period before the race begins? Having too much time can also turn into a distraction. The moment just before the starting gun of a race can be an extremely stressful period. Concentration becomes more difficult in sports because it must be done under pressure. Pressure can cause anxiety, and anxiety is a distraction. The stronger the anxiety, the shakier one's concentration tends to be. Worries, doubts, and self-consciousness can take over as attention goes into oneself and away from the task at hand.

The prevalence of anxiety and stress in sports points to the importance of relaxation. You concentrate best when you are calm. When you are reading a good book or involved in your favorite hobby, you don't have anything to prove. So even without your full awareness, the level of concentration can be quite deep. The same principle applies to sports. The state of calm, focused attention is crucial to good performance. So when you are training, focus on your breathing. Feel the energy of the other athletes around you. Become one with your footsteps or your bike pedals. Try to focus solely on your experience. Clear your mind of other thoughts and distractions. Glue yourself to what you are doing. Don't let it out of your awareness.

Once you're in this focused state, the pressure will subside. Pressure is the internal perception of an outside threat. When you concentrate, you build confidence in your skills and your ability to handle any threat. So whatever you were afraid of loses its power to upset your performance. Then all your focusing can be channeled into what you have to do right now. When you can stay in the present moment, you'll notice that you have more time to complete your activity.

Steps to Quiet the Mind and Deepen Your Focus

➤ Honor the power of silence, simplicity, and solitude.

➤ Use your energy and resources wisely.

➤ Live fully in the present moment.

➤ Cultivate an ongoing, open-minded inquiry process.

➤ Invite learning; make room for change and transition.

➤ Replace the word "problem" with the word "challenge."

➤ Find your rhythm and honor your own pace.

When you are physically prepared and mentally focused, you are ready for any challenge. Your finely tuned concentration can give you the edge needed to do your best in many situations. So focus your energies and go with your strength. Take a few chances and extend yourself mentally and physically. Then you won't spend time later thinking about what you should have done or what might have been.

Enhancing the Power of Your Concentration

Now let's do an exercise to improve your concentration. Here are three important skills to learn:

➤ Narrowing your focus to one object or thought
➤ Limiting your focus to the present tense
➤ Holding your focus for longer periods of time

Set aside 10 minutes each day to practice this technique.

1) **Create a relaxing environment:** Choose a quiet place to relax where you will be undisturbed (e.g., turn off your phone or pager, close the door, play some soft music).

2) **Practice deep breathing:** Begin by breathing slowly and deeply from your abdominal area. Choose a word that you can say several times to quiet the mind (e.g., "Relax," "Float").

3) **Choose an object of attention:** Close your eyes or focus on one spot in the room. Choose an imagined object of attention (e.g., a ball, someone in front of you, the finish line).

4) **Observe the object:** Mentally examine the object in detail (e.g., shape, color, size). Look at it from different angles. Feel the object; notice its texture. Listen to your object (e.g., hear the swimmer kicking in front of you).

5) **Intensify your focus:** Now intensify your focus on the object. See it, feel it, hear it, as though it were right in front of you. Maintain a passive attitude and you'll find your object will seem to come to you (e.g., see yourself getting closer to the athlete in front of you without any effort at all).

6) **Learn the feeling:** Once you have narrowed your focus, say to yourself: "My attention is totally focused on _____ . This is what it feels like to be fully concentrating."

7) **Re-focus your attention:** When your attention wanders and other thoughts enter your mind, just notice them, and gently bring the focus back to your object of attention.

8) **Reorient yourself:** Breathe deeply 10 times and gradually return your focus to the room, telling yourself that you feel fully awake and re-energized.

Chapter
11

Belief in Yourself: Managing Your Inner Critic

Your thoughts
create
your reality

Your mind is a thought factory: it produces 50,000 thoughts per day. Where your mind goes, your energy follows. How much of your training and your life is guided by negative or critical thinking? It is possible to direct your mind so that your thoughts are creating the reality you desire.

Within every athlete resides a negative inner voice that is primed to attack and judge you. It can make you nervous before important events, it can interrupt your focus, and it can keep you from doing your absolute best in training and performing. Most people have probably experienced the inner critic, but athletes are especially vulnerable to this negative energy in the high-pressure situations that are unavoidable in sports. Those with shaky confidence and low self-esteem tend to be more susceptible to a strong, debilitating critic within.

The inner critic has many faces and can influence your mind and body on many levels. The more aware you are of your critic's strategies, the better you can understand and control this negative energy. You can begin to train and perform with a mind that is clear and positive. Let's outline some of the inner critic's primary approaches:

Getting to Know Your Inner Critic

➢ The inner critic blames you for most things that go wrong. It holds you responsible for both the things you can and can't control (e.g., how your opponents perform at a competition).

➢ The critic sets unrealistically high standards of perfection and then makes you a failure for making the tiniest error (e.g., "I've got to win this competition; anything less will be a complete waste of time").

➢ The critic compares your achievements and abilities to those of other athletes and makes you appear less than adequate.

➢ The critic keeps a perfect record of your mistakes but forgets to remind you of your personal strengths and accomplishments.

➢ The critic has a rigid set of rules and "shoulds" that you need to live by and yells at you for being wrong if you move outside these bounds.

➢ The critic has favorite degrading names for you and will have you believe that all of them are justified (e.g., "You stupid, incompetent slug of an athlete; why couldn't you get under 40 min. for that 10K?").

> ➤ The critic magnifies your weak points, using superlatives to remind you that "You always screw up in races; you never finish anything on time; you're always late."
> ➤ The critic reads your competitors' minds and convinces you that they are angry, turned off, or disgusted by you.

Strategies of the Inner Critic

The inner critic is busy undermining our self-worth most of the time. Yet the voice is so engrained in the fabric of our thought patterns that we hardly notice its harmful effects. The critic is so smart and cunning that the attacks often seem justified and quite reasonable. This negative voice becomes a familiar part of our mindset. The critic is readily breaking down any good feelings we have about ourselves and often prevents us from performing our best in sport, at work, and at home.

The inner critic, unfortunately, is the voice that we most often believe. When you say to yourself, "I really blew that workout, I'm a real failure, my training is going nowhere," these statements have a ring of truth to them. This kind of statement is easily taken in by the mind. It seems normal to judge ourselves because we are so intimately aware of what we feel and do. But the inner critic gives us a very distorted impression of what went on and only looks at the negative side of things. Imagine how you felt in your first competition. The critic filters out any normal, reasonable impressions by screaming that you were a "fat, bumbling spazola who is not fit to enter another competition."

The critic is a master at destroying our self-worth. Thus a strong inner critic can be disabling to an athlete's performance. It can be more toxic to your emotional health than a severe trauma or loss. Pain and grief from past events do pass with time, but the critic can be with you always, finding fault, blaming, and judging until you do something to intervene, which we will get to shortly.

Another powerful technique of the critic is to speak to you in a type of shorthand. The critic might yell two words, "Stupid idiot!" But those two words may contain the memory of the thousand times your coach or parent complained that you were not motivated enough, or smart enough, or fast enough. The tapes are stored deep inside your mind, and those two words instantly bring the painful memories into the forefront.

The inner critic often uses images of past negative experiences to degrade your self-worth. When you're in the middle of a competition, the computer critic quickly sorts through your hard drive and brings up a video replay of the same race when you did it last year "and really blew it." Then it says to you, "Here you go again, becoming distracted, letting your competition get away from you in the critical moment, just like last year."

Although the inner critic appears to be quite strong and prevalent in most of us, its power is really an illusion. The habit of listening and believing the critic can become highly engrained. However, by increasing your awareness of what the critic is saying, you can learn to turn that switch off or refute its statements with a positive reconstruction. You can change the channel on your inner radio before it has a chance to undermine your attitude and self-worth.

Re-Directing Your Inner Critic

To disarm the critic, you must first gain an awareness of its presence. We are constantly engaging in an inner dialogue with ourselves. We perceive what is going on around us, interpret our experience, review past events, problem-solve, and consider the future. Most of the time this self-talk is necessary and helpful in understanding our environment. Within that inner dialogue lies our inner critic's running commentary. Arresting the critic in its cunning game requires a special alertness.

Notice when that voice is saying: "...another dumb mistake," or providing you with an image of past failures. Be especially aware of these situations:

➢ Places where you feel criticized
➢ Conversations where someone might be disapproving
➢ Situations where you have made a mistake
➢ Interactions with authority figures
➢ Circumstances where you risk failure or rejection
➢ Times when you feel hurt or someone is angry at you

Self-Awareness Exercise

In this assignment you will learn to keep track of your inner critic and how it affects your performance as an athlete. For one week, become as aware as possible of negative self-statements that arise. Develop a sheet with three columns:

1) Time of day
2) Critical self-statements
3) Positive reconstructions

Count the number and type of critical self-statements you notice each day. When a negative thought comes up, write it down, and note the time of day it occurs. Then, in the third column, write down a positive reconstruction – a way to consider the situation in a constructive, helpful way. For example your negative thought might be: "I'm never going to get faster." A positive reconstruction might be: "My logbook shows I am making small but steady progress."

Notice how you can begin to interrupt the continuous cycle of undermining thoughts and develop a more positive attitude, just through awareness.

Tools for Managing the Inner Critic

Now let's focus on specific techniques to disarm your inner critic, so that you can learn to gain control and harness that power in a positive way to improve your training and performance levels.

As you become more aware of your critic's strategies, you will be able to understand how to control this negative energy. You can begin to train and perform with a mind that is clear and positive. If you completed the self-monitoring exercise above, you are now more aware of your critical voice. As you analyze these thoughts, you can notice the pattern of attacks.

You may hear powerful self-statements from your critic, such as:

➢ "I have to perform perfectly in this race. If I do everything just right, I will receive approval from people."

➢ "I'm going to screw up in this workout anyway, so I won't bother trying."

➢ "I'm comparing myself to other athletes, and I end up feeling more inferior."

Each of us has certain negative themes that get played over and over in our minds. When you become acutely aware of your critic's function and expose its negative purpose, you can begin to disarm it and make it less believable.

Refuting the Critic's Message

Once you begin to realize your critic's negative purpose, you need a way to reject the old negative programming in order to move toward a more proactive and constructive mind-set in your training and performance.

When we were growing up, many of us received hundreds of critical messages from our coaches or parents, telling us we weren't good enough, smart enough, or fast enough. I worked with an athlete client whose father had repeated to him over and over: "You're a miserable failure. Why are you even bothering to try out for the track team? I guarantee you'll never make it onto the varsity team. You haven't got what it takes. The other guys are so much better than you."

After a while your own critical voice steps in and replays the same old scripts you've been hearing from others for years. You can get stuck in a performance slump and see no improvement until you can learn to refute your inner critic.

In my work with athletes, I have discovered a number of effective ways of talking back to your inner critic. You can experiment with each of the approaches below and find which ones work for you.

Thought-Stopping Technique

Each time you hear your inner critic, you can use a phrase to bring it to your attention and powerfully disarm it. You can simply say to yourself one of the following sentences:

> ➢ Stop this garbage!
> ➢ There's no truth to this stuff!
> ➢ Shut up!
> ➢ No more self-judgments!

It's often helpful to do something physical along with verbalizing your phrase, such as slapping your thigh, or snapping your fingers. So you might tap your leg, as you say internally: "Stop!"

The combination of physical movement and verbal expression wakes you up and makes thought interruption more likely. This strong activity breaks the chain of negative thoughts and prevents them from snowballing out of control. The key is to catch the critic in the beginning stages, before it has a chance to pick up steam. With continuous thought-stopping interventions, the frequency of the critic's assaults will be greatly diminished.

Consequences of Your Inner Critic

Another way to disable your critic is to think about the price you pay when it moves in. One of my athlete clients assessed the toll that her negative thoughts had on her training, her professional and personal life, and her sense of well-being. She noted the following consequences:

> ➢ I am afraid to be aggressive in my training and never push myself at workouts.
> ➢ I get defensive when I receive criticism from my coach.
> ➢ I feel anxious at race starts because I don't feel well prepared.
> ➢ I don't finish marathons due to lack of motivation.
> ➢ I avoid trying new skills in my workouts because I'm afraid I'll do poorly.

> I've lost a lot of sales opportunities at work for fear of rejection.
> I tend to be cold and aloof in relationships because I'm afraid people won't like me.

Now you can assess the personal cost of your own inner critic. Begin to develop a list of ways that your negative thoughts have affected your training, relationships, work, and lifestyle. Then summarize them into one simple phrase you can use the next time your critic attacks (e.g., "I refuse to give in to you this time. You've cost me…").

Affirming Yourself

Once you've silenced the critic, you need to put something else in its place or else the critic will quickly return to fill the void with further attacks. You must learn to reinforce your self-worth in order to fully disarm your critic. You need to replace the critic's voice with a positive affirmation of your own self-worth.

The critic would have you believe that you have to continually prove your value in life through outward behavior, such as fast interval times, great race results, and medals on the wall. So athletes often fall into the trap of chasing medals, trying forever to make the grade.

The reality is that our true value lies in our existence as human beings. As athletes we have all known hope and fear, love and loss, goals and disappointment. Just the joy of training should provide us with our self-worth, rather than trying to prove that we are faster or better than our competitors. This is our self-worth, our humanness.

Here are some positive statements you might say to yourself to calm your inner critic and affirm your self-worth:

> I value myself regardless of how I do in this event.
> I am linked to every other person in this race. We are all just trying to do our best.
> I am worthwhile because I am aware and fully alive on this earth.
> I am doing the best I can with the body I was given.
> I am living life fully one day at a time.

Try out these statements and then create some of your own. Find affirmations that are believable for you and that you can use to substitute for your critical voice inside. The more you affirm your self-worth, the quieter your inner critic will become. As you begin to believe in yourself, your training will become more enjoyable, and your performances will naturally improve.

Chapter
12

Meditation:
Training Stillness
in the Mind

*Attend to your
present experience
with a sense
of wonder,
appreciation,
and celebration*

Carlette Guidry, two-time Olympic gold medalist in the 4 by 100-meter relay, spoke about the meditation strategy she uses to focus before each race. In an interview at Stanford prior to the 2000 Olympic Trials, she related to me: "Just before I get into the starting blocks, I have certain key words I say to myself. I repeat them several times, and it helps me get into the right mindset to perform my best."

Over the past few years, an increasing number of athletes are looking toward meditative techniques to enhance the quality of their training, as well as their personal and professional lives. They often become more relaxed and focused in the process, which makes their workouts far more enjoyable and productive.

Disciplining Our Attention

Meditation techniques are best understood as methods of disciplining your attention. They involve the practice of uncritically attempting to focus your attention on one thing at a time, while clearing your mind of everything else. Meditation can be a powerful remedy for troubling mind states as well as a potent method for enhancing wholesome and healthful states of mind. You can sharpen your perceptions so you see more clearly what is going on while you're working out or competing, and make adjustments more rapidly.

Most people have little awareness or control of how long they pay attention to a specific event or experience. For instance, have you ever gone to a movie and missed whole segments as your attention wandered off to other concerns, fantasies, or even into drowsiness? The nature of the mind is such that it does not want to remain focused on a single entity. A myriad of thoughts come and go as you try to concentrate. Through meditation training you can learn to be more completely present in the moment. Temptations toward distractions will inevitably arise, but with practice you can quickly recognize them and bring your attention under control.

One must understand that the art of meditation lies not in simply focusing on one object, but rather in the attempt to achieve this type of focus. Each time you realize that your mind has drifted to other thoughts, you can choose instead to re-focus on the original object of your attention. So let's say, for instance, that you are doing a set of intervals on your bike, aiming toward a specific time goal. Every time you notice your mind drifting and the pace falling off, bring your focus back to your training form, your breathing, and your pace. The better you become at refocusing, the easier it will be to stay on your goal pace.

The Value of Meditation for Athletes

Once you practice meditation for a few weeks, using the techniques described in the following sections, you'll be surprised at the gains you can make both mentally and physically. You will begin to notice that:

➤ You can develop a calm, quiet mind, with focused attention.

➤ You are developing the ability to remain attuned to the present moment of training even while growing tired.

➤ You can accelerate the acquisition of new skills. For instance, you can maintain better form while moving fast.

➤ You have the ability to choose which thoughts you wish to focus on. It is not necessary to think about everything that crosses your mind.

➤ You will find it impossible to worry, fear, or hate when your mind is thinking about something other than the object of these emotions.

➤ Your habitual negative thought and perception patterns will lose their influence on you (e.g, "I give up too easily. I'll never be able to complete a 100 mile bike ride, or complete a marathon").

➤ Emotions and thoughts are not enduring. They quickly come and go through the mind. Even the most potent emotion can be managed if you focus on your breathing and the sensations in your body.

➤ Once you become aware of what is happening in the present moment, you will become more emotionally even-keeled. The extreme highs and lows will diminish.

➤ Meditation provides a self-tuning capability that allows insight into your progressively subtler mind and body states.

➤ You will strengthen the mind-body connection and draw more satisfaction from your training.

Evidence that Meditation Works

Those in Eastern religions have for many years realized the benefits of meditation, but most Westerners have approached this practice with some skepticism, considering it an untested method. Dr. Herbert Benson researched various meditative techniques at Harvard University to see if they could counteract the physiological effects of stress. His research demonstrated that with meditation: 1) electroencephalograph (EEG) brain wave patterns indicated increased alpha activity, a sign of relaxation; 2) oxygen consumption fell by 20 %; 3) heart rate and breathing rates decreased; 4) blood lactate levels dropped, indicating less stress; 5) skin resistance to electrical current increased fourfold - a strong measure of relaxation.

Benson's research indicated that any meditation practice could produce these physiological changes as long as four factors were present: 1) a comfortable position, 2) a quiet environment, 3) an object of mental focus or attention, 4) a passive attitude.

Meditation has been used successfully in dealing with anxiety, sleep disorders, obsessive thinking, eating disorders, and depression. It has also been quite effective in the prevention and treatment of heart disease, migraine headaches, high blood pressure, strokes, and auto-immune diseases such as AIDS. I have used meditation quite successfully in my clinical practice to treat these conditions in my clients.

Three Types of Meditation

Although there are thousands of unique styles of meditation, most techniques can be classified into three distinct categories: concentration, reception, and reflection. Concentration is the type of meditation that will initially be most useful for athletes. We learn to intensify and stabilize our attention using this type of technique. This method is accomplished by focusing attention on a single object or activity and gently returning to it whenever you notice that your attention has wandered. Traditionally this involves attention toward the breath, a mantra or repetition of words, or a specific mental element (e.g., patience in getting to the finish line). Individuals trained in the martial arts use meditation to focus on a particular movement form.

Though the particular object of attention may vary, the qualities of mental stability, awareness, and single-minded focus are the primary qualities being developed. The practice of meditation will help you develop the quality of introspective alertness which recognizes distraction and enables you to keep your mind on what you are doing (e.g., training at a certain pace for a specified period of time).

The second type of meditation is called reception. This approach allows you to give mindful, passive attention to whatever arises within your sphere of experience (e.g., Zen meditation). We have all experienced this feeling when we gaze into the sky at night, marvel at the expansive ocean, or feel completely satisfied as we cross the finish line of an endurance event. Receptive meditation can allow athletes to effortlessly attend to the totality of their experience with a sense of wonder, appreciation, and celebration. As you learn to use all five senses to fully take in your environment, you can develop a powerful capacity to examine and understand the deep nature of your experience.

With reflective meditation, the third category, you can learn to engage in analysis or contemplation of a question, principle, idea, or experience. For instance, if you are cross-country skiing out in the wilderness, begin to stretch your senses and absorb everything around you (e.g., notice how your skis move through the different textures of snow). In our day-to-day training, this type of meditation can provide a powerful tool for understanding and ridding ourselves of mental barriers that we may encounter (e.g., diminishing negative thoughts). It is a skillful means for helping us remove the perceptual blinders that prevent us from seeing our true selves and from doing our best. Then we can respond to life with greater wisdom.

Physical Profile of the Successful Meditator

Some qualities that indicate likely success for athletes in the practice of meditation include:

➤ Good attention skills
➤ Interest in one's internal subjective experience
➤ Willingness to self-examine without self-criticism
➤ Being open to alterations of consciousness
➤ Being open to the possibility of improving
➤ A genuine sense of awe and wonder toward life
➤ A strong sense of internal self-control

© John Segesta – Triathlete Magazine

Preparing for Meditation

To get the most from your time meditating and to ensure that the results you want are attained, you will need to address: 1) posture or body position, 2) attitude, 3) focus, 4) breathing, and 5) the time you have for meditating.

1) Establishing your Posture

Choose one of the following sitting positions that is comfortable for you:

➢ In a chair with your hands resting in your lap
➢ Cross-legged on the floor
➢ Japanese fashion, on your knees so your buttocks rest on the soles of your feet
➢ The yoga full lotus position (not recommended for beginners)

Sit with your back straight, but not rigid. Imagine that there is a helium balloon with a string pulling the back of your head upward. You can also pull your chin in slightly. Keep your shoulders down and relaxed. Allow the small of your lower back to arch. Rock from side to side, then front to back a few times, and establish the point at which your upper torso feels balanced on your hips. Close your mouth and breathe through your nose. Place your tongue on the roof of your mouth.

2) Attitude

Developing a passive attitude is perhaps the most important element in both relaxation and meditation. When practicing for the first time, many thoughts will come and go and you will have relatively short periods of clear concentration. This is to be expected. Maintaining a passive attitude means not being concerned about whether you are doing things correctly or whether you are achieving goals. Just say to yourself: "I'm going to do this exercise, and I'll just accept whatever happens."

3) Centering

Begin by closing your eyes and noticing the place where your body touches the floor or chair. What do you feel there? Then notice the places where your body touches itself. Do your hands or legs cross? Pay attention to these points of contact. Next, focus on the way your body takes up space. How much space does it need? Can you feel the boundary between your body and space? Become aware of this sensation.

© William Dunn

4) Breathing

Close your eyes, take some deep breaths, and become aware of the quality of your breathing. Is it slow or fast, deep or shallow? Notice where your breath rests in your body. Is it down low in your abdomen, in the midsection, or in your upper chest? Try breathing into your chest, then into your stomach, then into your lower belly. Feel your abdomen move in and out with each breath. Abdominal breathing is the best way to relax for proper meditation.

5) Time Frame

Aim at meditating for at least 10-15 minutes per day. As you become more comfortable with these techniques, you may want to extend this to 20-30 minutes twice a day, for optimal results. You can learn to do meditation within a few minutes. However, the benefits of meditation increase dramatically with practice. The degree of relaxation will deepen as your attention becomes steadier. You will become more proficient at living in the present moment.

Movement Meditation

Most athletes work out for many hours per week in their training without much awareness. Your training can now become a way of practicing concentration. The following exercise incorporates movement, breathing, and counting as a way of focusing attention.

1) Stand up and take several deep abdominal breaths. Feel your abdomen expand and contract with each breath. Mentally repeat the words "breathing in" with each inhale and "breathing out" with each exhale so that your mind and body are working together.

2) As you begin your training, notice your breathing in relation to your body. See, for instance, how many footsteps or arm strokes you take naturally during each inhalation and exhalation.

3) If you are running, count your steps in time with your breathing as you run. For instance, if you take 3 steps per breath, you could say: "In...two...three. Out...two...three." Your in breaths may be longer or shorter than your out breaths. Additionally, your step count may vary from breath to breath depending on the terrain you're running and your pace. Just pay attention and readjust your breathing as needed.

4) When other thoughts or images interrupt your counting, simply make a mental note of this and return your attention to your form, breathing, and counting.

5) A different way of practicing this technique is to pay attention to the sensations of your physical activity. Do a whole body scan. If you are walking or running, notice which muscles contract and which ones relax as you push off with each foot. Which part of your foot touches the ground first? Pay attention to how your weight shifts from one foot to the other. Are your arms relaxed; do they swing easily from the shoulder and elbow? How do you hold your body? Is it straight up or leaning forward? Are your shoulders too high or tense? How do you hold your head? Is it held too far back? What happens to your form when you get tired? Also pay attention to the ground in front of you. What is its texture? Do you see any cracks or stones? Become aware of your thoughts; then let them go. Notice everything.

Mantra Meditation

The mantra is the most common form of meditation and is quite easy to learn. Select a word, syllable, or phrase that you would like to use. It may be a word that has meaning for you (e.g., speed, energy, or flow). Or it may be two nonsense syllables that sound pleasant. You could use the word "one." Many prefer the universal mantra, "OM."

1) Select your posture and center yourself while taking several deep breaths.

2) Chant your mantra silently to yourself. Say the word, phrase, or syllables over and over in your mind. Whenever your mind strays, take note and bring your focus back to your mantra. Notice the sensations in your body. Let your mantra find its own rhythm as you repeat it over and over again.

3) If you like, try chanting your mantra out loud. Let the sound of your voice expand as you relax. Notice the difference in how your body feels.

4) Realize that meditation must be practiced with awareness. It should not feel mechanical, as this may lead to falling asleep. Try to remain aware of each repetition of your mantra.

Now that you know the basic techniques, practice meditation on a daily basis. Mediation opens the mind to the greatest mysteries that take place in our everyday lives. It widens the heart so that you may feel the eternity of time and infinity of space with every workout. It can give you the perception that you are moving in paradise while living on earth. So during your next workout, stop thinking so hard. Look at the world around you as if you had just arrived on planet Earth. Use meditation to become aware of everything within you and around you. In time you will notice your performance improving, and your training will become a far more pleasurable and meaningful activity.

Part
IV

Performing
With
Intention

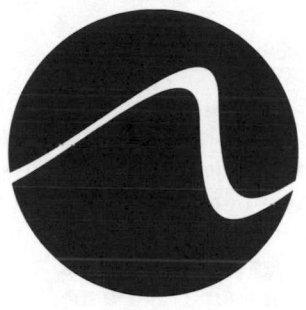

Chapter 13

Understanding Performance Anxiety

Nervousness can be your best ally; harness the power from your nervous system and direct it toward your goals

Have you ever become so worried or anxious before a race that it hindered your performance? Athletes who consistently perform well have found ways to re-channel their negative thoughts, take charge of their emotions, and turn their nervous energy into a powerful source of inner strength and confidence. They have developed the ability to quickly shift from a negative focus to a more constructive stance within their sport as well as in other aspects of life. Becoming aware of your anxiety level and emotional state is critical to doing well in any event. Only then can you properly direct your energies away from self-consciousness and toward a great performance.

To become an Olympic gold medalist, an athlete has to train for the pressure as well as for the event. I had the opportunity to interview Stacy Dragila just before she won her gold medal in the first-ever women's Olympic pole vault competition in 2000.

World champion and world record holder, Stacy Dragila talked about her high anxiety level prior to the Trials and the Olympics. While training for the Trials, Stacy said, she became aware of increasing nervousness. She told me, "Even day-to-day tasks would bother me and make me anxious." Stacy chose to deal with the problem directly.

She went to her Idaho State assistant coach and asked for his guidance. She told him: "I'm worried that I'm not going to make the opening height. I'm concerned that I'm not going to qualify for the team." Then she began doing relaxation and imagery exercises. She worked on acknowledging her fears and then letting them go. She told me: "I would go into a quiet room and close my eyes. I'd see myself relaxing and doing the perfect jump." After practicing these techniques regularly, Stacy felt she was better able to handle the pressure and was ready for the Olympic Trials.

When you worry about your performance, the anxiety is manifested in both physical and cognitive forms. This same response system occurs whether you are making a speech at a business meeting, involved in a job interview, worrying about an upcoming confrontation with your spouse, or driving to an important race. A high level of stress can cause you to blank out on an exam or forget the name of someone you have known for years when introducing them to an important group of people.

Our bodily responses are quite similar even though the precipitating circumstances may be quite different. We not only worry in our minds; our whole body worries. If you are concerned about having a difficult conversation with your boss and you picture it in your mind, your body responds exactly as if you are right there in that confrontation. You may notice sweating or an elevated heart rate. We always experience some reaction in our body that accompanies our mental state.

Whenever worry comes into play, we often experience a disruption of focus and dysfunction of ability to perform to some degree. In athletics we sometimes refer to this as "choking." This leads to making mistakes and critical errors in your sport (e.g., Dan O'Brien not clearing the opening height in the pole vault at the Olympic Trials in Atlanta).

Learning the Warning Signals

The good news is that our bodies provide us with a multitude of warning signals that we are getting out of control.

Some of the obvious mental cues include:

➤ Lack of focus
➤ Forgetting critical details
➤ Sense of confusion
➤ Resorting to old habits
➤ Inability to make decisions
➤ Rapid speech

Some of the physical signs of a high stress state include:

➤ Hyperventilation
➤ Muscular tension or muscle twitches
➤ Elevated blood pressure or high heart rate
➤ Irritability or sense of fatigue
➤ Cottonmouth or unsettled stomach
➤ Visual distortion or flushed face
➤ Diarrhea or need to urinate

Most of us have some combination of these symptoms when we get nervous or scared about not performing well on a particular task. If we had all these symptoms at once, it would signify a panic attack. But most of the time, we experience only a few signs at any one moment.

When I have my athlete clients use my computerized biofeedback system, I notice that each of them has his or her own individual response pattern to stress. Some people respond more with their cardiovascular system, which may lead to high blood pressure or rapid heart rate. Other people have a more reactive respiratory system that can cause problems in races, with short, shallow, nervous breathing and dizziness or hyperventilation. Still others have an over-reactive muscular system and may be more prone to neck and shoulder pain and tension, headaches, or leg cramping. Some people have a combination of these systems all over-working at once.

Individuals vary in how much their performance is affected. Therefore, it is critical that you identify which responses you associate with anxiety and notice whether they influence your performance in a positive or negative way.

What Produces Anxiety?

Worry often occurs when there is a difference between what is hoped for or expected, and what is actually happening. Let's say you go to a race, primed to do your fastest sprint triathlon time ever, and you encounter pouring rain and 25 mph headwinds. Your knee starts aching during the warm-up, and your team is counting on you to do a fast time to get the critical points needed in the race series.

Chances are, with these conditions you're not going to be turning out a personal record and will need to change your goals. But the external pressure is still there. You need to be able to read your mental and physical stress cues (listed above) and interpret them correctly. Notice if your arousal level is too high. You can then intervene early, before the stress becomes too unmanageable. You can learn to take deep breaths, do some positive self-statements, and relax enough to problem solve and re-adjust appropriately to the situation.

Good Arousal vs. Bad Arousal

It's important to distinguish between being worried and being psyched and ready for the challenge of competition - what we might call "good arousal" and "bad arousal." Bad arousal is generated by fear and nervousness about performance, feeling out of control. Good arousal comes from enthusiasm and feeling ready for anything. Only you can determine what causes your arousal and how high or low your level of energy needs to be for optimal performance.

Another factor that leads to worry and anxiety is being overly concerned about the outcome of your performance. Not knowing the outcome and obsessing about all the "what ifs," can threaten your sense of well-being. When you concern yourself with the consequences of the outcome, the worry can turn into a stifling fear.

You may be thinking, for instance, "If I don't perform well in this one race, I'll lose critical points in the race series, I'll let my team down, I won't get asked back to the race, I won't get any media exposure, I may well lose my sponsorship." Those are powerful negative thoughts that can certainly affect your mental outlook and the way your body performs.

Tools for Handling Performance Anxiety

Athletes who consistently perform well have found ways to re-channel their negative emotions, take charge of their thoughts, and turn their nervous energy into a powerful source of inner strength and confidence. With the tools discussed in this section, you can learn to quickly shift from a worried mind to a more confident focus within your sport as well as in other aspects of life.

Recent research and self-reports from top athletes suggest that virtually all performers experience high levels of pre-competitive anxiety. Many even have extremely elevated anxiety levels. Even with these high levels of nervousness, however, many athletes perform exceptionally well and very close to their potential. So it appears that the determining factor is not how much anxiety is there, but how the athlete perceives his or her own personal signals of anxiety and how they are channeled.

Interestingly, the literature shows that for elite athletes, pre-competitive anxiety is manifested primarily on a physical level. The cognitive or mental manifestations of anxiety are largely absent. So difficulties such as forgetting critical details, a sense of confusion, inability to make decisions are not major problems for top athletes. This may be one distinguishing factor between those who consistently do well in races and those who continually fluctuate.

In the absence of any cognitive disruption, most elite athletes can focus and direct all their energy toward the task at hand. They simply disregard the physical signs of anxiety and understand that butterflies in the stomach, for instance, are part of being excited and ready for the race. So you can say to yourself, "Ok, I'm nervous, and this is the way I feel when I race my very best. These feelings are associated with great performances."

Assessing Your Stress Response Pattern

Now you can learn to harness this power from your arousal system and direct it toward your goals. You can have all that energy working for you instead of interfering with your performance. Let's look at some ways of achieving this objective.

First, you can learn about the elements of your specific stress response system through keeping an accurate logbook. By recording how you feel mentally and physically throughout each workout and race, you can determine your exact optimal performance profile and begin to reproduce it in each event you do. You can record the race outcomes and assess your stress level in each one. Then you'll learn the exact arousal state that leads to a great performance.

Here's how to keep a log of your stress responses. Generate a chart by writing five categories across the top of a page:

➢ Stress response
➢ Workouts
➢ Pre-Event
➢ Competition
➢ Evaluation of Performance

Then, on the left side of the page in the "stress response" column, list the ways you personally respond to competition, both mentally and physically. For example, you might list some of these: butterflies in stomach, muscle twitches, rapid breathing, racing heart rate, dry mouth, sense of confusion, lack of focus, trouble making decisions, forgetting details, irritability, desire to urinate, or yawning.

Then you can keep track of the frequency and intensity of these responses each time you work out and compete. Rate each of the responses from 1 (None) to 10 (Very intense) for your workouts, pre-event, and competition so you know how strongly you react. Then evaluate your workout or race in the final column by rating it on a scale of 1 (Magnificent) to 10 (Lousy).

Now you can develop a profile of which responses, at what intensity, correlate with your best performance. Each person has a unique response system, so it's important for you to find out what particular arousal pattern works for you.

> Dan Poynter, author of *Parachuting: The Skydiver's Handbook*, talks about anxiety and high-risk situations: "In the sport of skydiving, there are a number of possible emergencies; happily all are rare. But you must be educated in these areas; you must be properly prepared. The point is that we do our best to learn and to minimize the risk. However, skydivers think differently. They look for the risk/excitement; they pursue it. For example, in a tornado watch, most people take cover. A skydiver will drive to get as close as possible to witness it."

Remember, you are an active participant in regulating your arousal state. You can develop the ability to feel and experience what is going on in your body and mind, and fine-tune your energy level to achieve your ideal performance state. Then the excitement you experience can be viewed as a positive and powerful energy source that will serve to maximize your talent and skill.

Re-Channeling Nervous Energy during a Competition

Here are some additional tools you can use on the spot to remain cool, calm, and focused in the heat of battle:

Breathe Deeply: The quickest, most efficient way to relax and get centered before a race is to take 10 slow, deep abdominal breaths right at the starting line. As you inhale, you can say to yourself, "I'm breathing in strength." With each exhale say, "I'm breathing out tension." That way your body and mind are in complete synchronization.

Accept Nervousness as Your Friend: Just accept the fact that you're going to be nervous. That is a normal reaction before any important event. You can make this feeling your ally rather than fighting with it. In fact, nervousness is a good sign that you're excited and ready to roll. It's important to distinguish between being worried, and being psyched and ready for the challenge of competition. Tell yourself, "This feeling is directly connected to doing my best. The more I feel this way, the better I'll perform." Once the gun goes off and you get moving, the nervousness will subside. You can just relax and enjoy the ride.

Remind Yourself That You're Well Prepared: Think back on all the great workouts you've completed to prepare for this race. Look over your logbook in your mind. Remember how dedicated you've been and how far you have come in your training. Tell yourself: "I'm well-trained, rested, and ready to do my best."

Mentally Rehearse the Event: Go over in your mind exactly how you would like to do your race. If you have time, visualize several possible scenarios so that you're prepared mentally to respond to anything that might come up. For example, see yourself in the lead, coming up from behind, racing alone, or feeling tired and getting a second wind.

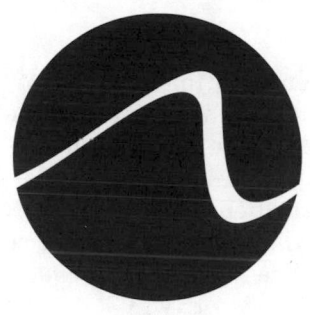

Chapter
14

Dealing with Pain
and
Negative Energy

*Mental toughness
is a muscle
that needs exercise,
just like the muscles
of the body*

Mark Allen, six-time winner of the Hawaii Ironman Triathlon, has always relied on focusing strategies to empower his mind to handle adversity. I had the opportunity to interview Mark, and I asked him about his mental preparation. He told me: "Every race is a teacher. Each time I tried to win the Ironman I became more focused and more mentally tough. I've learned that even in difficult situations, there are many different ways to win."

Winning the Ironman did not come easily for Allen. He did not finish his first race in 1982. In 1983 he finished in third place. In 1984 he had a 12-minute lead during the run, but then became dehydrated and had to settle for fifth. He came in second to Dave Scott in the 1986 and 1987 races.

The race in 1989 was a turning point for Allen. He explained to me: "Dave Scott had won the Ironman six times before. In '89 I raced side-by-side with Dave Scott for 140 miles. When you're with someone hour after hour, you can sense his energy. I could tell the guy was rock solid. There was nothing I could do to intimidate him, so I had to outrace him. After eight hours we were still running together; we had two miles to go. I told myself, if I'm still with Dave when we get to the last hill, I'm going to focus all my physical and mental energy and take him on the uphill. With one mile to go, I put the pressure on and finally won the Ironman for the first time."

Even the finest competitive athletes occasionally find themselves struggling with negative attitudes or becoming too focused on physical pain during training or racing. Like the rest of us, they strive to keep moving forward in spite of negative beliefs and internal chatter that plague the mind as they attempt to challenge their limits. What distinguishes the best athletes, however, is their acute ability to manage and control that negative energy. Top competitors have developed the ability to relax, remain positive, and maintain focus under tremendous pressure and physical challenge.

Consider the scene at the 1996 Summer Olympics in Atlanta during the men's 100-meter track finals. The world's top sprinters were subjected to immense pressure. Athletes who had trained for years were primed to render their best performances, but they were met with a series of mishaps and distractions. They had only 10 seconds to offer every ounce of anaerobic energy their bodies could produce. Three false starts began to drain the precious strength in their legs, and for some, the dream started to drift away. Linford Christie made his second false start and protested his disqualification in a lengthy tantrum, and then began parading around the track, causing 100,000 confused fans to boo or cheer.

You saw the growing frustration of the world's greatest sprinters: anxious, angry, pacing, and wondering how much longer this circus would go on. They were thinking: "Which sprint will be the real one that we actually get to finish - the one that determines the gold medal and perhaps my future?"

But there was one athlete who was not pacing. He didn't seem disturbed by the whole fiasco. Donavan Bailey sat calmly, smiling, appearing to be meditating. He was not wasting time worrying about things he could not control. In fact, he was conserving energy and building inner strength while the others were depleting their resources. Sure enough, when the final sprint began, Donavan Bailey was ready, using the whole sequence of events to his advantage. He shot out of the starting blocks like a bullet and ran 9.84, setting a world record. He had channeled all of this external negative energy into the best possible outcome.

No matter how well-trained you are or how refined your athletic skills become, you will inevitably encounter some situations that seem physically painful or mentally challenging. The key is to recognize them early and to develop strong mental skills with which to intervene. Let's explore some primary warning signals:

Typical Signs of Negative Energy or Pain:

- Anxiety or fearfulness
- Tunnel vision
- Difficulty concentrating or thinking clearly
- Diminished emotional control
- Self-defeating beliefs and self-critical thoughts
- Accelerated heart rate, with short, shallow breathing
- General aching or body pain
- Weakness in the arms or legs
- Muscle tension or cramps
- Sense of events occurring in slow motion or at an accelerated rate

Everyone has probably experienced a few of these symptoms at some point during their training or competition. With regular practice and awareness you can manage pain and let go of negative energy more effectively. You can control how deeply you feel things and how long feelings and moods last. You can learn to shift from one emotion to another and change your focus from physical or mental discomfort to the intensity and enjoyment of your sport.

When managing pain, we need to first distinguish two different types: bad pain and good pain. Bad pain is the type that can be potentially injurious. It is often a sharp pain in a joint area, like the knee, hip, ankle, or back, which, if it persists, should be checked out by a health professional. Good pain is the type that builds strength while not doing physical damage. It is the feeling of heart, lungs, and muscles working hard. This is the type of discomfort that you can work through, using your mental training techniques. Now we'll explore how to use mental imagery and other skills to manage pain and dispel negative energy.

Tools for Handling Good Pain and Bad Energy

1) Relax mentally and physically. Deliberately slow down and deepen your breathing. This will help your muscles let go, and you can relax through the pain. Say to yourself:

"I'm breathing in inner strength; I'm breathing out negative thoughts."

"I'm becoming more relaxed with each step."

2) Break the experience down into smaller, more manageable pieces. If you're doing the Ironman, don't think of getting to the finish line from the gun. That's much too far away. Just say to yourself:

"I'm now focusing on swimming to the turn-around point."

"Just get to the first aid station on the cycling leg."

"I'll hold this pace one more mile, then see how I feel."

3) Use the pain as feedback. You can register it not as pain but as effort level. Say to yourself:

"Now I know exactly how hard I'm working; I know how this pace feels."

"My body is doing what it should be doing."

"This is how I should be feeling in order to improve and go faster."

4) Redefine the pain as just a sensation. Say to yourself:

"Oh, I have felt this sensation before; this is familiar; I can handle it again."

"This feeling is connected to doing my best and being focused."

"Last time I felt like this I did a personal best."

"I'm experiencing the same sensations in this competition that I have practiced in my training."

5) Put your pain in another context. Distance yourself from this sensation so the relationship you have to the pain can change.

Imagine yourself as an external observer watching yourself performing well in your sport.

View yourself from a camera lens; you can zoom in or zoom out to distance yourself and make the discomfort seem less intense.

6) Embrace the pain. Rather than avoiding the pain, you can draw it closer. Say to yourself:

"If I just hold on to this feeling a little longer, I can perform the best I have ever done."

"I am learning to enjoy this feeling of intensity; it helps me focus."

7) Associate. Be fully in the here-and-now, completely aware of your body and the task at hand.

Do a body scan every few minutes to assess your form and technique.

Ask yourself questions: "How are my legs feeling? What is my turnover rate?"

First contract and then relax any problem muscle groups.

8) Disassociate. Go somewhere else in your mind. Do this when you are not at a critical point on the course where you need full attention.

Imagine yourself swimming with dolphins or soaring like a bird.

Visualize yourself doing another sport which you enjoy (floating effortlessly, smoothly).

9) Develop a self-chant or a mantra. Create a simple set of phrases or words that you repeat to yourself to help you stay focused and prevent negative thoughts from entering. You can say:

"Smooth, easy, efficient."

"I believe in myself; I am well-prepared for this event."

Count your breaths or footsteps.

Sing your favorite song.

10) Create a sense of fun and enjoyment. Remind yourself of how much you enjoy doing your activity. If you can come from this perspective, the negative energy will quickly diminish. Say to yourself:

"I am doing exactly what I want to be doing."

"My body is getting stronger and faster every moment."

"I am in my element."

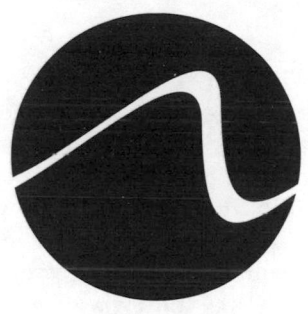

Chapter
15

Embracing the Challenge: Putting It All Together on Competition Day

Sometimes all you need to do is walk through the door that has been opened for you

Time is running out. The big event is one week away. The whole season boils down to this next event; you can feel the pressure mounting. You feel physically prepared, but what about your head? How do you react in demanding situations? If you've prepared mentally and physically as we have mapped out in the previous chapters, you won't need to worry much about pressure. In fact you may go out of your way to put yourself in pressure situations. You'll be the type of athlete who thrives on a close race, a tight match between you and the person in front of you.

Pressure is something you put on yourself when you're not prepared, when you don't have faith in what you're doing, or fear the unexpected. Now you have a choice. You can look forward to the challenge of the race and test your limits, or you can cringe in front of it. When I talk with clients coming up on an important event, my advice is to welcome pressure. Look at it as an opportunity to shine, to celebrate your fitness and your sport. If you embrace the competition and thrive on it, you'll be amazed at how successful you'll be. When the situation gets tight, you'll have the edge. You'll know there's just as much pressure on everyone else, and you'll know exactly how to handle it.

When I work with athletes preparing for an important competition, I often hear common concerns about performance anxiety, self-doubt, and difficulty relaxing as the event date draws near. They are often so focused on the physical elements of the race that they forget to prepare emotionally for the real race inside the mind. When race day finally arrives, often something comes up that they weren't mentally prepared for, and it can throw the whole race plan off course. Here are some of the most extraordinary sources of pre-competition stress and distractions. Choose your favorite excuse.

Top 10 Competition Day Excuses

10) The alarm didn't go off (I set the PM instead of the AM), my car was running on three cylinders, I got to the event late, and my warm-up didn't go smoothly. Actually it was non-existent.

9) I was so hungry and nervous at the carbo-loading dinner, I ate too much pasta and bread the night before the race.

8) My normal pattern was disrupted by a noisy hotel, a lumpy mattress, not enough sleep, traffic delays getting to the event, and receiving an unlucky race number, so I just lost it.

7) At night I found myself worrying about the race outcome, obsessing about the points that I needed for the race series.

6) I had a fight with my spouse the night before, and my boom box got thrown out the window with my favorite pre-race CD!

5) It started raining two minutes before the gun went off, and I slipped on a Power Bar wrapper.

4) I was on a personal record pace, but my shoelace came untied in the last mile.

3) I was feeling great at mile 18 until I had to relieve myself; there were thousands of fans surrounding both sides of the course and no bathroom in sight.

2) I was so ready for the race physically, but mentally? Well, I had to be taken in to emergency counseling the night before the race.

1) My dog peed on the directions to the race start, and I ended up at a lawn bowling match.

> Michael Johnson gave his post race interview after winning both the 400 and 200 meters and breaking his own world record in the 200 at the 1996 Atlanta Olympics. He said: "I had so much pressure on me to win that race, with huge contracts at stake, wearing Nike's golden track shoes, and all the predictions that I would be the first man to win a double at the 100 and 200 in the Olympics." In fact, with all the pre-race hype, he even stumbled at the start but still managed to smash his own world record in the 200 meters. Rather than being stymied by the pressure, he turned it into positive energy and used the situation to propel his body forward to a whole new level.

Michael Johnson did not let excuses get in the way of meeting his personal goals. He embraced the opportunity to shine and realize his potential. Now let's talk about a specific plan that you can use to mentally prepare for your upcoming races.

The Sequence of Mental Preparation

Three Weeks before the Event

Athletes often ask me, how early should you mentally prepare for a race? Each person is different, but there is no such thing as starting too early. You need to be practicing mental training techniques as an ongoing part of your training. When competition time arrives, you're just putting on the finishing touches. Generally, a good time to begin specific mental preparation is two-three weeks prior to the event. The main objective in this phase is to build confidence by mentally rehearsing the race in its entirety. Use the tools of visualization and concentration described in earlier chapters. Spend ten minutes each night before bedtime doing relaxation and mental imagery of the upcoming event. Build on your past successes in training by capturing those feelings of fluidity, power, and effortlessness. Experience yourself as composed, focused, and competent. Include in your daily visualization a simulation of all the extraneous possibilities that might occur during your event (create your own "top ten list"). See yourself responding to the unexpected in a constructive manner, being able to handle any circumstance.

Three Days before the Event

Now the majority of the preparation has been done, and there is little you can do physically at this point to improve your performance that day. However, you can easily overtrain too close to the event and sabotage your ability to perform well.

Athletes often find it difficult to switch gears and allow the body to rest. The best use of your time during this period is to train mentally, which can make a significant difference in the outcome. There are some vital concerns that need to be addressed in order for you do your best. As you are reducing your physical training by tapering down, you should increase the time you spend in mental rehearsal. Don't wait to do all your mental training until the night before the event.

You also need to gain greater control of your surrounding environment (e.g., reduce your work load and get more sleep) so that you can allow your internal self to focus on the job ahead. The idea is to develop a sense of contained excitement where you feel eager and yet under control. You are storing energy so that when the right time comes, and when you give the word, you can let your body explode into action.

The Night before the Event

Now the real focusing needs to begin. Take time to develop a pre-race ritual or pattern that you carry out in the same way before each important event. A familiar routine reduces anxiety and helps one feel better prepared. It minimizes fear of forgetting something at the last minute.

Here are some important pre-race strategies:

Visual Models: Watch a video of athletes competing in your sport. Expose your mind to athletes with good form for ten minutes before bedtime; then incorporate this into your mental imagery exercises. The fluid motion of these experienced athletes will gradually become programmed into your brain and muscles.

Quiet Time: Take ten minutes to do abdominal breathing, and mentally rehearse the race in its entirety.

Triggers: When something is a trigger for anxiety, turn it into a signal for relaxation.

Distractions: Watch a light comedy or inspirational movie to divert attention from the race.

The Right Clothes: Wear the clothes that you wore when you had your best race or workout. Wear whatever makes you feel successful and gives you a winning feeling.

Eating Smart: Maintain your regular eating program. Eat familiar foods that work for you at a scheduled time before the race. Don't experiment with new, exotic, or spicy specials on the menu.

Environment: Find what works for you - being around friends or being alone - to feel more at ease.

Pre-race Checklist: Arrange for travel, set the alarm, develop a list of things to bring and do (e.g., bring race number, fill gas tank, pack water or sports drink, bring race shoes, bring pre-race, during-race, and post-race clothing, etc.)

Nervousness Is OK: Don't get anxious about being anxious. It's perfectly natural to be nervous before an important race. Some nervousness is unavoidable, and it may actually contribute to your best performance. Say to yourself: "These pre-race jitters are an indication that I am really 'psyched' to do well."

The Right Energy: Do whatever makes you feel good to achieve an emotional and physical high for the race (e.g., call a good friend, play your favorite music, complete a creative project, take a Jacuzzi or massage). Avoid activities that are likely to make you tired, sad, upset, depressed, or negative (e.g., avoid personal conflicts, horror movies, high workload, upsetting relationships, etc.).

Now you know what to do three weeks before, three days before, and the night prior to the competition. We've talked about how to thrive on pressure, how to use visual models of success, how to handle distractions, and how to achieve the right emotional state to be ready for your race. The kind of mental preparation we have discussed here is critical to maximizing your potential in an upcoming event. Unfortunately, there are no crash programs to help you do your best in your sport. You can read books, get advice, and watch the pros, but you must practice both physically and mentally if you want to really gain an edge.

Michael Johnson set the world record (43:18) for the 400-meters, at the 1999 World Track and Field Championships in Seville, Spain. On the night before that race he said to himself, "Ok, this is a perfect environment. I have a wonderful opportunity here; make use of it. All the factors are in place: good weather, great crowd, and an excellent track. This is really good timing. I'm healthy, well trained, rested, excited, and ready for action. I ran 44 seconds and something last year when I was injured. Now this year I'm healthy, so I know I can go much faster."

Now we'll discuss the keys tools for putting it all together on race day. I'll show you how to be mentally tough on race morning, through the race start, and all the way to the finish line and beyond. I'll give you specific strategies to use throughout the race and afterward which will make a real difference in your performance and self-confidence. I'll describe how you can turn every race into a powerful learning experience regardless of the outcome.

The Morning of Your Event

Your primary concern during this important phase is to quiet the mind and regulate the flow of adrenaline so that you can achieve your optimal level of arousal. Athletes are very individualized on this issue, and what works for Michael Johnson may be totally inappropriate for you. Some athletes do their best while highly energized; others need to be more relaxed. You need to find your right level of energy. Keep a detailed post-race log for each race to find out what emotional state works best for you. Here are some suggestions for regulating your level of arousal for your event:

Music: Play your favorite music tape or CD while traveling to the race, one you associate with success.

Arousal adjustment: If you are too anxious, do deep abdominal breathing; if you are too unmotivated, clench your fists and take a few short, rapid, deep breaths. Do some quick movement; dance to the music.

Familiarity: Follow your usual pre-race routine, don't try anything new, and carefully attend to last minute details.

Quiet the mind: Following your warm-up, go to a quiet place, breathe deeply, calm your mind, and remind yourself of how well prepared you are (e.g., say to yourself: "I have done this a thousand times before; I am fully trained, well rested, and ready to do well." "I perform well under any conditions").

Lighten up: Enjoy the event (e.g., take your mind off the race for a few moments; think of your favorite comedy scene; tell a joke to a friend; remind yourself that this is just another race, not a life or death situation).

Oxygen supply: 30 seconds before the start gun, take ten deep breaths to relax and improve mental clarity, and to increase oxygen supply to the muscles.

The Start

So the gun goes off and it's time to put it all together. You can now let go and enjoy the feeling of speed and energy flowing through your body. However, you may need to deal with a number of distractions throughout the event such as fatigue, pain, fear, and unexpected race conditions. You have a multitude of tools to work with that we've discussed in previous chapters. Now you can put them to use in a high intensity situation:

Focus on your immediate goal: Break the race down into manageable pieces and begin to focus only on the first portion, not the entire race (e.g., say to yourself: "I'm just relaxing and getting my rhythm during the first mile").

Stay in the present moment: Remind yourself to stay in the here and now; let past and future events fade into the background.

Focus on the process not on the outcome: Look only at what you need to do right now (e.g., pace, breathing, concentration); your final place or time will take care of itself.

Intensify attention to your form: Do a body scan and relax your tight muscles frequently. Ask yourself: "Are my shoulders and neck relaxed? How does this pace feel? How much energy is left in my legs or arms?"

Handle the pain: If you have "good pain" that is not seriously damaging your body, just shift attention to your breathing or cadence of movement, and let the discomfort fade into the background.

Use everything in the race to your advantage: For example, if another athlete passes you, tuck in behind him and go with his energy for as long as possible. You may catch a "second wind" and be carried on to a new personal record.

Use imagery throughout the race: Visualization is not something you do only in the quiet of your bedroom. Now use your images to create feelings of speed and power (e.g., when you come to an unexpected hill, visualize a magnet pulling you effortlessly to the top).

Be aware of distractions: Breathe out unwanted thoughts with your next exhale and re-focus your attention instantly on what is important.

Make positive self-statements continually: Negative thinking is quite common; everyone has an inner critic. Become aware of these thoughts early on. Don't fight with them; simply acknowledge their presence, and then substitute a positive affirmation (e.g., you're thinking: "This hurts too much; I want to lie down and die"). Say to yourself: "This feeling is connected with going faster and doing my absolute best."

Celebrate your fitness and strength: Let your body do what you've trained it to do. Remember that your goals are realistic. All you need to do is perform up to your capabilities.

Post-Competition Critique

After you reach the finish line, it is critical to evaluate your emotional and physical experience before, during, and after the event. Your place and time are only one type of feedback. Most athletes overlook many other important elements. Now that the race is over, you can learn a great deal through a careful analysis and by making detailed entries in your logbook. You can be doing continual research with each race, finding out what emotional state and energy level work best for you. You need to examine the meaning of your performance and put it into proper perspective. You often learn the most from a less than optimal performance, which can provide valuable strategies for future competition. I have found it's best to wait until the day after the event to more fully and objectively evaluate the outcome. Do a written post-race critique, and ask yourself the following questions:

➤ How would I rate my mental and physical preparation for this race?
➤ What did I learn during the race that may help me in my next event?
➤ Was I sufficiently rested mentally and physically before the race?
➤ What was my race strategy, and did I actually use these tactical plans during the race?
➤ At what point did I start feeling fatigued? When did I feel the most tired?
➤ What mental tactics did I use during the difficult points in the race?
➤ Was I able to fully concentrate throughout the event?
➤ What tools did I use to handle distractions (e.g., deep breathing, mental imagery, focusing, affirmations)?
➤ What are my goals for my next event, and what do I need to focus on now in my training?

Now that you've seen the entire pre-race sequence, you can start planning for your next event. But remember, no matter how well-prepared you are, you may still find yourself caught in a difficult race situation, with self-doubts creeping into your thinking. This is quite normal, and there's no need to panic. The way this is handled is what separates Tegla Loroupe, Lance Armstrong, and Tiger Woods from the guy who drops out of the race. The secret to their success is that they know exactly how to handle these moments. They know they can't avoid them. So when they pop up, they don't lose it; they handle them. They slow down, they take a few deep breaths, they go back to the very fundamentals of their sport, and they focus.

By concentrating intensely on what you need to do at that moment, you can block everything else out of your mind and allow the self-doubts and the fears to fade away. Then you can free your body to do exactly what you've trained it to do. Instead of working so hard, you can just float and dance. Let the race become a true celebration of your internal strength and fitness.

Affirmations for Relaxing through a Race: When you want to quiet your mind during a hard race, you might ask: How can I be exerting effort and relaxing at the same time? Actually, most great performances occur while an athlete is feeling calm and at ease. Without muscle tension or pressure, it's easier to extend one's limits.

So first practice relaxation in a resting position. Once you have mastered this technique, you can try relaxing both mentally and physically while you're in action. To see results in races, you need to practice relaxation during hard workout efforts. During each interval on the track or the road, concentrate on releasing muscle tension by letting go with each exhale. Say to yourself: "I'm breathing in energy, I'm breathing out tension; I'm breathing in focus, I'm breathing out negative thoughts."

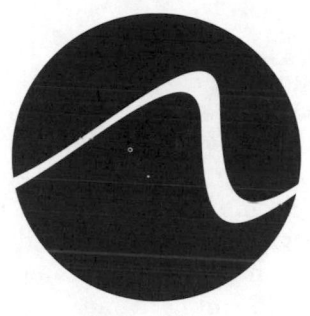

Chapter
16

Lessons in Excellence:
Losing and Learning

*Success comes
in many ways,
one of which
is winning*

Greg Louganis, the champion diver, is the only man to do a gold medal sweep in all five diving events at the same Olympics. However, his road to victory was not the conventional route. On his first dive, Louganis hit his head on the board going into the water. He remembers the event vividly during an interview: "I felt this thud on my head. My first feeling was embarrassment. How am I going to get out of the pool like this without people laughing at me." After having five stitches sewn on his head, he immediately got back up on the board. He said: "As I looked out to the audience, I patted my chest. The audience sighed as if to say, we're scared for you too. I felt that they were with me." Louganis then proceeded to win gold in this and the next four events.

Have you ever done one of your worst performances at a time when it was critical for you to do your best? Perhaps you were prepared to peak in an Ironman Triathlon and win your age division, but the circumstances did not allow for that to happen. Major losses in racing and in life have a way of playing with our self-esteem. We tend to be most susceptible to feeling down when we expect to do well at a competition and end up with a poor outcome instead. The consequences can lead to anxiety, self-doubt, self-defeating thoughts, and even long-term depression. These disappointments can be devastating, but there is no reason they need to be. To lose is to be human. Everyone who thinks, feels, and lives experiences loss. No one can escape it, not even the world's champion athletes. The important thing is to make the transition from a difficult loss to ultimate gain as quickly, smoothly, and painlessly as possible.

Winning or meeting your goal is easy to accept in a competition. However, athletes who want to be successful learn to accept disappointments as well. Losing can be far more beneficial in the long run if you learn to properly re-examine your goals, assess your training program, and make necessary adjustments. Few athletes take the time to analyze what led to a successful performance. However, falling short of a goal can force you to take a good, hard look at what went wrong, and determine how to avoid the problem next time around.

No one enters a competition with the aim of losing; you hopefully compete with the attitude of being successful. In time however, you come to accept that winning is only one of many ways to succeed. In endurance sports you can have the greatest race of your life and still lose the contest.

Setting Process Goals

To put your performance in the proper perspective, you need to set process goals and evaluate them on the basis of progress rather than outcome. So you might, for example, set a goal of maintaining good training form and concentrating for longer periods of time than in the previous competition. This goal is well within your control and can be objectively evaluated. If you set realistic process goals and carry out a consistent plan to meet them, the results will take care of themselves.

I once worked with a top masters runner, John, who felt that winning the masters division was the only outcome he would accept. He embarked on a heavy race schedule chasing medals and victories. Whenever he took second place, he would regard this as a failure. John would compensate for his loss by over-training for the next race to the point of injury. After a while he began to ask himself, "Is this all there is?"

During our sessions I helped John learn how to evaluate his accomplishments in ways other than outcome alone. Once he could perceive that there are several avenues to success, his enjoyment of the sport was greatly enhanced. After placing second in a race he could grow from the experience and establish new goals that eventually led to greater personal satisfaction and better performances.

Approaching Loss from a Different Angle

Losses in races can be an opportunity to find out something that is difficult to learn under any other circumstances. You can say to yourself: "I really screwed up this time; all those hours of training have been wasted; I let all my friends and family down." Or you can approach the situation with a more forgiving attitude. You can say: "All right, so I came up short on my goal. This doesn't mean I'm a worthless person. I am disappointed, but this is not a life or death situation. This has nothing to do with my value as a human being. It has to do with performing a specific skill, under particular conditions, on this particular day. Ten years from now this one experience will probably appear insignificant in the whole of my life."

Then you can ask yourself, "What positive lessons can I learn from this experience that will help me to improve my performance under comparable circumstances in the future?" You might say, for example: "I can get better rest during the entire week preceding the race; I can do deep breathing to relax at the starting line; I can warm up on the last mile of the course so I know what to expect at the finish line."

All great athletes have failed at some point, and the successful ones have learned to turn their losses into eventual gain. Failing to meet their preset goal can be frustrating, but they don't regard this as a catastrophe. They determine that on this day, this particular strategy didn't work, or that their fitness wasn't where it was last year, or that they need to work on concentration. They don't destroy themselves over a poor performance. They use it as an opportunity to become stronger and better prepared for the next event.

Being Open to New Options

Falling short of a goal can lead to frustration, distress, and feeling hopeless. It can also be the best thing that ever happened to you. It can give you a chance to really get to know yourself and challenge your ability to cope with adversity. It can help you re-evaluate what is important in your life and reflect on what direction your training is taking. You might even decide to choose a new event or a different sport.

> After winning the San Francisco Marathon in a time of 2:43, the author lost two subsequent races and developed a stress fracture. During her six-month lay-off from running, she decided to take up swimming and cycling to cross-train and recover. This new interest led to exploring the sport of triathlon. The next year she went on to finish 2nd woman overall in her 1st Hawaii Ironman Triathlon, a talent she may never have discovered otherwise.

The road to satisfying performances is often a roller coaster of progress and setbacks, peaks and plateaus. If you do lose in a race, remember that the loss is not the sum total of your life; it is one experience that you are presently going through. Your life is much bigger than this loss. The disappointing feelings will fade, and you can emerge from the experience as a stronger, wiser person. Your athletic abilities may well flourish from it.

So take risks in your training and racing to test yourself and experience life to the fullest. You may not always perform your best, but in time your realistic goals can be achieved. The better you can adapt to your successes and failures, the more satisfied you will be. Take care not to measure your self-worth only by the race results. Don't worry about chasing after others' approval; do it for yourself.

Generate your own guidelines for success and strive for progress, not perfection. Enjoy and appreciate the journey, not only the final event. View setbacks as a challenge to strengthen your inner resources, an opportunity to learn about yourself and grow. Then you can turn every loss into a gain and put yourself back in charge.

> Winning becomes hollow without an understanding of the effort and progress you have made to produce the outcome.

Making the Best of a Bad Race Day

Now let's put these principles into practice, and you can see how you would handle a difficult race situation. How do you hold up in the heat of battle when things are not going as planned? Let's say you have set lofty goals for your next race, and you are primed to run your best 10K in a long time. You get to the race, put on your shoes, and begin to warm up. But instead of being springy and light, your legs feel like lead. As you run a couple of miles, they begin to loosen up, but you know the energy is not there; this may not be your day. You try to keep your chin up and stay motivated to run well. But in the back of your mind you are questioning whether you should be competing today.

The gun goes off; you begin your first mile. The other runners are pushing and crowding around you. It's hard to move, and you're just trying to keep from falling over. The first mile goes reasonably well, and you begin to get into a rhythm. You're actually running on target race pace for the first mile. You are thinking, "God, I'm in great shape. I'm up here with these great runners. If I can just stay with them, I may be able to win my age group."

Mile two arrives and the magic is over. Your legs are tightening up, and you're barely maintaining the same pace through an incredible effort. At mile three the runners around you start to pull away. You attempt to keep them in sight, but the harder you try, the more they slip away. You reconsider your goals, move into a more reasonable pace, and aim to hang on for the rest of the race. However, at this point you have trouble motivating yourself to stay competitive in the event.

Your Plan A in this scenario was to run a personal record and to win your age group. That goal is no longer realistic at this point in the race. Now it's time to move to Plan B. The question is, do you have a Plan B at this critical moment? Knowing how to shift your thinking when things are not going your way can make all the difference in your performance and consequently how you feel about the experience afterward.

I often work with athletes who set very high goals, but then have no backup strategy to switch to when things don't turn out as planned. To become a successful athlete you need to take into consideration all the possible scenarios and see yourself as owning the tools to handle any situation. You can visualize yourself as having a great day, having a so-so day, or having a lousy day, and decide what you will do to perform your best in each situation. That way, regardless of what happens, you'll have a way to make it a positive experience.

Now in our earlier example there were several possible elements, both internal and external, that could influence your race. Let's go through some hypothetical situations and see how you might handle each of them.

Scenario A: You're in terrific shape, feeling like former world 800-meter record holder Wilson Kipketer, flying through each mile as though it were no problem. You can focus on reeling people in who are in front of you, pushing the pace on the last half of the race, and going for the sprint at the finish line. You meet or exceed your racing goals in terms of time or place. When you are having the perfect day, you can just relax and enjoy it. Let your body do what you've trained it to do.

Scenario B: You're not feeling quite up to par on race day. Your initial goal was to run a 10K personal record and place in your age group, but your pace is slowing after two miles, and you're unable to stay with the top group. You switch to Plan B - You say to yourself: "When the next runner passes me, I'll tuck in behind and use that energy to maintain my pace and break the wind in front. I'll maintain that pace as long as I can. If the runner pulls away, I'll tuck in behind the next person who passes and let him or her pull me along." You can use these affirmations to keep yourself motivated: "This race is making me stronger for the next one." "I love to run this distance." "I am in my element."

Scenario C: You're feeling lousy, and you can't even come close to your planned race pace. You go to Plan C - You keep your watch going and continue to take your splits. However, it may be best not to look at them if you feel the times are too discouraging. You can review them later. You can then say to yourself: "OK, I'll just focus on maintaining good running form, stay competitive, and try to do the best time I can, given my fitness on this day. It will still be a good training run and will help prepare me for my next race. I can make this a positive experience no matter what happens." Your positive affirmations may include: "My body and mind are growing stronger every moment." "I feel grateful that I am healthy and able to run at this pace." "I am using the energy of the other runners to carry me along." "I will just try to stay with the runners who are keeping my pace."

Scenario D: There's howling wind and pouring rain on race morning. You switch to Plan D - Have the wisdom to separate the things you can't control from the things you can. Use the wind to help you lean forward and improve your running form. Look for tall runners to draft behind. You can say to yourself: "I can't change the weather or the other runners." "What I can control is my own running form and my attitude." "Everyone out here has to contend with these same conditions." "I know I can handle this situation."

Try mentally rehearsing each of these scenarios; then generate your own versions. If you anticipate what might come up for you and develop a plan A, B, C, & D, you'll always have a response to any problem that may arise. You will be prepared to make the best of all your race situations.

© John Segesta – Triathlete Magazine

Interview with Dave Scott, Six-Time Winner, Hawaii Ironman Triathlon

One of the best examples of how to handle a bad race day comes from Dave Scott's experience in the 1996 Hawaii Ironman. Here is a personal account from the Ironman winner.

JoAnn Dahlkoetter: Dave, tell me about your greatest moment as a triathlete.

Dave Scott: Many people remember me for being the Ironman champion. I won the Hawaii Ironman in 1980, '82, '83, '84, '86, and '87. But the race that means the most to me is the 1996 Ironman. The '96 race was more satisfying than all my previous wins. That was the epitome of mental attitude carrying me through a very difficult situation.

JD: You had also competed in the 1994 Ironman?
DS: Yes, I was 40 years old then, and I placed second.

JD: That was a major achievement at that age. Why was your 1996 race so special?
DS: I was two years older then, and my training time was much more limited. I have three kids, and I do a lot of coaching. So every minute of the day was scheduled. With all the business and family demands, my workouts were more psychologically draining. I also had more pressure, since I had placed second in 1994. There was no withholding of comments and expectations from outsiders. I felt I was fitter in '96 than in '94, but the problem was I had overtrained for the '96 race.

JD: Take me through your '96 race.
DS: The gun went off and we dove in the water. I had a horrific swim; I was well back in the field, two minutes slower than in '94. A sea of masters and women finished ahead of me. I came out of the water in 19th place and felt flat. I was about to begin the bike ride, so I had to use my psychological strengths. Going back into my memory, I pictured myself doing my absolute best training ride. I felt invincible. On that day, on that training course, I won. There was no one but me out there.

JD: How important was this race to you?
DS: I considered the '96 Ironman the biggest race of my life; it would be the end of my competitive career. But the race was not developing as I had planned. My legs felt heavy on the bike. I was talking to my legs, trying to get my breathing going. I kept saying to myself, "They'll come around; they always come around."

No one had gone by on the bike of any consequence. Then a few people went by me. I had never been in this position before. I couldn't believe how bad I felt going by the airport, only 30 miles into the bike ride. The psychological part kept chipping away at me. I felt terrible. The NBC van would go by; you could see the look on their faces. I know they must have been thinking, "Oh, Dave, you should have quit two years ago. Hang it up, Dave, your time is over." I remember seeing my family planted on the course. I would hear, "You're 10 minutes behind the leader, 12 minutes behind, now 15 minutes behind." It was mentally staggering. I must have said to myself 1000 times, "Let's just give this up and pack it in." But I kept riding.

JD: How did you turn things around?

DS: Something happened at 80 miles into the bike ride. A little voice inside me said, "Hold yourself high; just do the best you can. People will still respect you for what you have already done. Your family is not going to leave you." At 80 miles reams of people were going by on the bike. I felt like I was riding on flat tires. But I said to myself, "Just wait until I get to the run. I'm confident I can run 2:40-something in the marathon. No matter what happens on the bike, I know I can turn it on in the run. And I can finish the last 30 miles of this bike ride."

That was the turning point for me in the race. From there on it became a mental game. I was out there all by myself. Then I saw my wife on the course. I asked her, "Where is 10th place?" I've always been in the top 10 in the past. Me wife told me how far I was behind number 10. I decided that was going to be first place for me.

Getting off the bike and pulling into the transition area was devastating. I was in 26th place. I had never been that far back before. But I said to myself, "Wait, I am going to turn this engine on like you've never seen before." I know I can have the flattest day on the bike and then turn around and have a great run. Starting the marathon, I felt a tremendous psychological gain. To me, that's when the gun went off.

JD: How did the marathon go for you?

DS: In the first mile of the run, I caught four people. I was running under six-minute pace for the first six miles. I remember catching the 14th person. It brought me back to my strengths in previous years. I saw myself running smoothly. In reality, I know I'm the least smooth runner out there. But who cares? I can't see the TV cameras. All that matters is how I'm seeing it.

I remember catching a German guy as I moved up to 10th place. But between miles 15 and 18 I felt flat. The German pulled up ahead of me again. That's when I caught my second wind. My mental clarity at that point was the best ever. My senses were especially acute. I moved up to number nine, then eight, then seven, and then six. At 24 miles I re-caught the German and finally finished in fifth place. I thought, "This is phenomenal; this is the greatest day of my life!"

Visualization Exercise for Receptivity: Reflection on the Lake

Find a quiet place, close your eyes, and begin to breathe deeply. Picture in your mind a calm mountain lake, a serene body of water held in a receptive basin by the earth itself. The lake you see may be deep or shallow, small or large. Note in your mind's eye that the lake seeks its own level; it asks to be enclosed and held. Sunlight sparkles in the lake's ripples and dances on the waves.

Notice that when the lake is calm it reflects clouds, trees, and rocks; it mirrors everything in itself temporarily. As the wind stirs up waves on the lake, the reflections disappear. When the sun sets, the moon appears to dance on the lake along with the outline of trees and mountain shadows.

Now, let yourself become part of this quiet mountain lake. Allow your energies to be held by your awareness, in the same way as the lake waters are held by the accepting hands of the earth. As a tiny wave rolls up on the shore, take a deep breath in. As the wave moves back out, exhale fully. Allow the pattern of the waves to match the rhythm of your breathing.

Allow your mind, body, and spirit to be open and receptive to whatever comes near. Feel the absolute stillness when both the reflection and the water are clear. Notice the difference when the surface is disturbed and choppy. Reflections can drift away for minutes or even hours.

As you continue to breathe deeply and meditate, enjoy the play of different energies of your mind and body. Experience the momentary thoughts, images, and feelings, which come and go just like the ripples and waves of the lake. Notice what effect or value they might have on your state of mind. Examine the range of energies moving on the lake—the reflections of shadows and light, the wind and waves, the colors of the sun and moon. Do your feelings and thoughts disturb the surface of your mind? How do they affect you? How does disappointment or losing an event cause a rippling of your spirit? Can you see a choppy, uneven surface as a crucial, fundamental part of being a lake?

Let your awareness now take you beneath the lake's surface. You can become the stillness below the surface as well. Notice that now you feel only a gentle rocking, even when the top of the lake encounters a powerful storm. Likewise, can you appreciate not only the substance of your thoughts and ideas, but also the enormous pool of awareness below the surface of the mind?

Now as you look in the mirror of the lake, view your own reflection. Make it your intention to acknowledge all of the qualities of the body, mind, and spirit, accepting both the wins and the losses of life, just as the lake is supported and contained by the earth, reflecting the sun, moon, stars, birds, and trees. The lake is content to accept the passing of the seasons, which bring out its vitality. Nature continually offers repair and preservation. You can become one with the lake, being reflective, maintaining total awareness and attention, and having the courage to be with what is.

© Victah

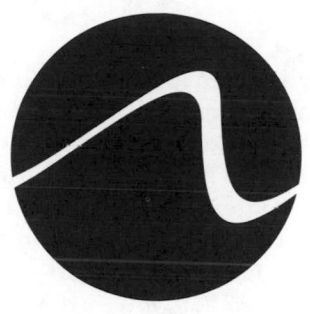

Chapter
17

Preventing Performance Slumps, Injuries, and Burnout

Persevere even through the lowest periods; you will arrive at a new equilibrium

lthough physical activity is often pleasurable and meaningful, there will inevitably be periods when interest wanes, energy diminishes, and you feel like you're going nowhere fast. You find yourself just going through the motions as internal pressure builds, boredom sets in, and workouts appear more like an obligation than a pleasure. Each training day seems endless, when the only "pleasure" is the conclusion of the exercise. When you lose motivation and fall into a rut, the hazards of performance slumps, injuries, or burnout may begin to slowly appear.

For most athletes, training provides a sense of self-confidence, a feeling of control over life, and the opportunity to test personal limits and reach new goals. However, when goals become unrealistically high, internal pressure builds, making workouts more like a duty than a pleasure. When this happens, you may become desensitized to your body's feedback and unknowingly over-train, creating serious risk for injury or burnout.

Sports like running, swimming, and biking are effective ways of handling so many needs that for some athletes, training may become an all-consuming pursuit that preempts all other interests in life. Having a focused commitment to physical improvement is by no means harmful in itself. However, when you become so attached to your sport that it becomes the sole means for coping with life, its positive effects can quickly diminish.

Slumps are Universal Experiences

In working with athletes as a sports psychologist and coach, I have frequently heard comments like the following: "I'm recovered from my injury, but I can't seem to get my form back." Or "I'm at 100 percent physically, but the motivation just isn't there." I've heard people say: "I'm working harder than ever, putting in more time training, and there's absolutely no progress," and "I've been training so well for the last few months, but now suddenly I'm stale. My legs feel dead. Is it something in my head?"

If any of these statements sounds familiar, take heart – you are not alone. Plateaus and slumps are universal experiences that all athletes and performers have gone through, regardless of ability level or type of sport. The experience of peaks and valleys is normal, but there are ways to ensure you experience more high points than low ones.

Dan Jansen struggled with his position as the best speed skater in the world for several years without having won an Olympic gold medal. Every four years, when the opportunity presented itself, something would happen. At the Olympics in Norway, after slipping and missing his chance at a medal in his first event, he finally relaxed. The next day he said to himself, "OK, this is my last event. I'm just going to go out there and skate, and enjoy what I'm doing." Taking the pressure off himself and letting go of the outcome allowed him to move out of his slump and capture the gold medal that had eluded him for so long.

Anyone who has challenged himself or herself for a long time has probably experienced a period of frustration. How long this period lasts depends largely upon your ability to recognize the symptoms and intervene early.

The Type A Profile

The athletes with a high risk for injuries, slumps, or burnout often show classic Type A personality characteristics: they're high achieving perfectionists who are independent, have a strong need to be in control, find it difficult to relax, and are not expressive emotionally. If your training pattern fits the following description, you may be unknowingly setting yourself up for disappointment:

Tunnel vision: You tend to avoid developing a broad-based lifestyle, with social support, a variety of interests, and a firm sense of self. You cling to your training as your primary coping mechanism and use exercise to deal with most of life's stresses.

Chasing goals: You use your athletic goals as a way to continually prove yourself, but are rarely satisfied - even when your goals are reached. You are constantly looking toward the next target, but can't relax and enjoy the journey.

Obligation: You feel you must complete the daily mileage in your program, regardless of weather conditions, personal state of health, or enjoyment level. Training becomes a duty.

No pain, no gain: You continue to train through pain that worsens during a workout - a sure road to injury or loss of motivation. Athletes often get into trouble by testing pain thresholds on a daily basis. Many athletes are afraid to rest because they have trouble changing gears. They can't relax and trust that their body will remember what to do.

Repetition: Doing the same activity over and over, week after week, with little or no variation can bring about a sense of boredom or declining interest. Even if physical injury doesn't affect your enthusiasm, then mental strain can eventually take its toll.

Seriousness: With the demands of a rigid training schedule and the pressures of competition, you can lose the element of fun in your workouts. Building more enjoyable periods into a training routine is critical for preventing burnout.

Self-inflicted wounds: You frequently condemn yourself for failures, setbacks, and mistakes rather than realizing they are inevitable and may offer good opportunities for learning.

Avoidance: You become overly anxious about meeting a goal; this may lead to subconsciously wanting out. A sick or injured athlete doesn't have to face the pressures of the real competition.

The Stress Connection

Once you're caught up in this pattern of obsession and over-training, stress can easily set in and hamper training, making you more prone to injury or burnout. Let's say you're not prepared for an upcoming race and feel anxious about it. Agonizing over the event creates more pressure and can often lead to physical and psychological responses that hinder performance. This defensive posture makes the body more prone to muscle and tendon strains. Blood shifts away from the extremities, and the leg flexor muscles may contract unnecessarily. Anxiety interferes with the ability to concentrate, which raises the chances of injury or accidents occurring.

After an injury or slump sets in, you must contend with even more stress that can interfere with healing and recovery. Being injured or feeling burned out is, in itself, stressful. Not being able, or not wanting, to exercise can bring on the withdrawal effects of depression, anger, or anxiety. You begin to ask yourself, when will you regain your previous level of fitness and excitement about training.

During a slump, the abilities that you once possessed can almost seem to disappear. For example, the triathlete loses precious time in the swim-bike transition of a race. The tennis player continually double faults on the serve. The championship golfer can't even get the ball onto the putting green. In every sport, slumps and down periods are common, natural elements of training.

If you are seeing signs of mental fatigue or body strain stemming from a rigid, repetitive schedule, it is a good time to reassess your situation and perhaps make some changes.

Evaluate Your Risk for Burnout or Injury

After working with athletes of all levels and noticing common areas of stress, I have developed an evaluation system to assess the chances of mental burnout or injury. A yes answer to four or more of the following questions is an indication that you may be at risk for a prolonged slump, injury, or illness:

> ➢ Do I feel locked into a routine?
> ➢ Have I trained too long or too hard in a high-pressure situation?
> ➢ Do I have a progressive loss of enthusiasm, energy, or sense of purpose?
> ➢ Does my normally comfortable pace feel difficult?
> ➢ Do my legs feel heavy or fatigued longer than usual after training?
> ➢ Do I dread the thought of training?
> ➢ Am I becoming more cynical?
> ➢ Is it difficult to get out of bed in the morning?
> ➢ Is my appetite below or above normal?
> ➢ Do I have excessive weight gain or loss?
> ➢ Do I feel mentally fatigued or irritable?
> ➢ Do I have physical distress: minor pain, headaches, or sleep problems?
> ➢ Do I have physical or emotional exhaustion?
> ➢ Am I becoming sullen or withdrawn?
> ➢ Do I have an angry, negative attitude?
> ➢ Do I have a diminished belief that I will be successful?
> ➢ Am I more susceptible to colds, or do I have shortness of breath?
> ➢ Is my resting heart rate or exercise heart rate higher than usual?
> ➢ Do I have frequent minor accidents as a result of inattention or stress?

Indeed, loss of pleasure and burnout are major barriers that can prevent you from training consistently, year round. But you have to wonder, is it even advisable to strive for maintaining a high level of motivation throughout the year? Attempting to be "psyched up" and in top form at all times is a sure path to staleness and burnout. Breaks and variations in the routine are crucial for long-term enjoyment of your sport.

Below are some strategies that may help you build variety into your life and create renewed interest in your training.

Staying Motivated and Preventing Burnout and Injuries

Follow the seasons of your sport: Many activities have natural yearly cycles, especially winter sports like skiing. Synchronize your training and peaking to your sport's competitive season. Other sports like running occur year round, and thus it's best to create your own seasons.

Establish a wide variety of objectives throughout the year for your training. For instance, you could establish four phases of the year that would include base building, strength/speed, peaking/competing, and rest/recovery. Each stage can bring you up to a higher level of fitness, or you can divide the year into different types of training or competing in different sports.

Seek intrinsic rewards: Develop a sense of internal value and meaning for your training. Build self-confidence during those times when external rewards are not forthcoming. Begin to appreciate the positive changes that training brings. Notice the exhilaration created by your body's endorphin production and the sense of total health and well-being. Develop a positive body image from building a stronger physique. Notice the psychological benefits: stress reduction, improved concentration, and greater self-worth.

Build in variety: Many athletes train with a small, fixed number of workouts (e.g., every Wednesday is track – 800's or mile repeats; every Sunday is the long run or bike on the same course, at the same pace). You may be starving for change in your routine. Any kind of variation is bound to create more motivation and interest. Try changing one element of your training each week. Go to a new scenic trail or park at least once a week. Alternate hard and easy days rather than working out at the same pace every day.

Try exercising at different times during the day and discover the period when you have the most energy. Put new spark in your schedule by incorporating different types of training: interval work, tempo (faster) workouts, fartlek training (variable speeds), hilly workouts, and endurance work. Take a day off and do a cross training with a different sport. There are endless combinations if you use your imagination.

Take regular breaks: Short, medium, and long-term breaks are all necessary to maintain your motivation levels. Try taking a one-day break from training each week, and take three days once a month. Then allow a week's rest after each major phase of your training (every three months). Take two-four weeks off once per year or after a major competition. During that time, try "active rest" by doing a different sport (e.g., skating, hiking, swimming, cycling, cross-country skiing). You'll get a tremendous psychological boost and probably not lose any of your fitness level.

Your break time is also a good opportunity to give attention to other aspects of your life. Build a broad-based lifestyle with a variety of interests. Strive for a balance between work and fun, social time and personal quiet time, and time to be creative. Do projects and hobbies at home that give you satisfaction. After your break you'll be mentally and physically rested and performing better than ever.

Go on a sports vacation: Sign up for a summer camp where you can discover new places to train, learn more about your sport, and connect with new faces, or plan your own healthy get-away and go to some place exotic to run, bike, swim, hike, and relax. While you're on vacation, bring more playfulness into your workouts. Leave your watch back at the hotel and do a workout just for fun without having to time or score your efforts.

Stopping Then Re-starting an Exercise Program

Whenever you need to take a break from training due to injury, mental fatigue, or other priorities in life, coming back can be a challenge, physically and psychologically. Follow these steps to ensure your steady progress:

Be honest with yourself: Stop the wishful thinking and write down exactly where you are right now: current mileage and training pace. That way you have a definite starting point and can progress from there. Do a full assessment of other commitments in your life that require your time and energy (e.g., job, new infant, longer commute). Then decide how much time you have to devote to your training (e.g., workout, stretch, cross-training, travel time).

Take the pressure off: Don't try to force your physical improvement. Lighten up on your rigid training schedule and exercise according to how you feel each day. Remove the strict deadlines or competition dates you've been pondering. Let your next breakthrough occur naturally, at its own pace, when the internal conditions are right.

Use setbacks as learning opportunities: When coming back from a lay-off, it's easy to condemn yourself for past failures, setbacks, and mistakes rather than realizing that they are inevitable and offer excellent opportunities for learning. Do the best that you can do, draw out the constructive lessons from every workout and race, and be able to move on. Look for advantages in every situation, even if the conditions are less than ideal.

Set realistic goals: Don't consider competing until you're reasonably fit. Choose an event perhaps four to six months after you've begun training. Competitions can be discouraging if you jump in too soon and are not fully confident and ready. Chart your progress in training and note every small step forward. Give yourself gold stars in your logbook for those stellar achievements.

Get connected: Develop a network of close friends and family. Join a fitness club or find people to train with who are similar in ability. The positive energy of other athletes is contagious and will keep you fired up.

Avoid comparisons: Instead of looking back on past times, try to set personal records for each new season. Start fresh and shoot for the best possible performances you can do this year. Try different courses for your speed workouts so you won't have any past times with which to compare.

Be grateful and enjoy the moment: Take each day that you are able to work out as a victory, regardless of the pace. Make a deliberate effort each day to create enjoyment in your sport, renewing your enthusiasm and excitement for training. Do the best you can with the fitness level you are at today.

The challenge is to create a healthy, balanced training program with enough variety to keep the motivation high and boredom low. You need to discover that point of pushing just hard enough, without going over the edge in training and in other areas of life. Try putting these mental training techniques to work, and you can learn to live more fully, train more healthfully, and feel exactly the way you want to feel.

Mental Training for Professional and Personal Life

When performance declines in any area, most individuals try to force themselves back to their previous output level. Business people work even more hours, while athletes train even harder - leading to more worry, tension, and pressure. They unconsciously intensify their frustration, causing it to last even longer.

The way to turn the slump around is to slow down and become aware of what is happening in your life. Close your eyes, take in some deep breaths, and listen to your own natural rhythms. Get back in touch with your true self and pay attention to your energy level. Rather than resisting the slump, think of it as a valuable warning signal, a message that something is out of balance and needs changing. Go with what your intuition is telling you. Don't fight your way through the plateau. Relax through it, be gentle with yourself, and open yourself up to the opportunity of learning. Trust that in time, things will turn around.

© John Foss

Tips for Rising Out of a Slump

Fatigue: If you are feeling physically or mentally tired, avoid fighting your body's messages. Instead of trying to stay awake with coffee or sugar, take a short relaxation break or nap. Yield to the tiredness and give your body the rest that it needs. In 15-20 minutes you'll feel renewed energy that will last throughout the day. You will also bring your body into proper balance.

Conflicts: When you feel friction between yourself and another person, and you've held your feelings in for a long time, you can easily sink into a slump and feel stuck. Instead of covering up your feelings, learn to express them assertively, as each issue arises. You don't need to be aggressive or forceful. First, listen carefully to the other person's opinion. Then, when you speak, you can come from a place of understanding. The two of you can clear the air and arrive at a mutually acceptable solution. Your relationship will be deepened and you will feel stronger inside.

Work: Notice how you manage your time, and be conscious of over-scheduling. Does your appointment book become full as you schedule more and more activities to be done in less and less time? Do you have a vague sense of guilt if you are not doing anything? Do you display polyphasic behavior – engaging in at least two to three activities at a time (e.g., driving while talking on the cell phone and eating a sandwich)? Notice if you have a rushed attitude about your work. Do you hurry through each activity during the day? While standing in the quick check grocery line, do you impatiently examine the cart ahead of you to see if they have too many items? To avoid burnout, take deep abdominal breaths often and allow for some down time in between each activity in order to recharge the body, mind, and soul. Trust that things will be completed in their own time.

Posture and Personal Energy: Notice if you carry excess muscle tension throughout your body. Do you experience dysponesis - using more muscles than are necessary to complete each task? Do your neck and shoulders ache at the end of the day? Become aware of your face and voice. When conversing, do you finish other people's sentences? Notice if you speak explosively - raising your voice or accentuating key words. Do you use fast, jerky, or emphatic gestures or hostile facial expressions?

If so, try this exercise: See if you can go through each movement during a day using the minimal amount of muscle tension possible. Hold the steering wheel of your car as lightly as you can. Write a letter using only your fingers, not your shoulders. Speak to an employee in a gentle, affirming way. Then notice how much energy you have at the end of the day.

Breathing for Healing and Recovery from Workouts
This exercise combines the relaxing effects of complete breathing with the healing power of self-suggestions and imagination.

➤ Sit or lie down comfortably and begin deep breathing through your abdomen.

➤ Imagine that with each inhale, healing energy is rushing into your lungs, and with each exhale this energy is flowing out to every cell in your body. Visualize a clear picture of this energizing process.

➤ Now, put one hand on an area that is sore or tired or injured. With your next exhale imagine that this healing energy is flowing directly to the area that needs special attention. Then inhale more energy. As you exhale, imagine this energy is stimulating and healing the injury, and driving out the pain or irritation.

Affirmations for Preventing Slumps and Burnout

- ➢ I am learning how to pace myself throughout each day.
- ➢ I am listening to my body; I honor its need for rest and recovery.
- ➢ I know when to push myself and when to hold back.
- ➢ My body and mind are flexible; they can switch into many different gears.
- ➢ I know how to take good care of myself.

Affirmations for Healing from Injuries

- ➢ The more I rest, the quicker I am recovering.
- ➢ I take full responsibility for my injury and for my health.
- ➢ I forgive myself for my part in this injury process.
- ➢ As I rest, there is a wonderful process of healing going on within my body.
- ➢ This experience is teaching me more patience every day.
- ➢ I now fully appreciate my health, my body, and my training.
- ➢ I am growing more motivated every day to fully recover.
- ➢ Every day I am growing closer to doing what I love to do.
- ➢ I have gone through this healing process before (with other injuries); I can do it again.
- ➢ This recovery period is a relatively very short time in the whole scheme of things.
- ➢ I have a strong support system of friends and family to help me through this situation.
- ➢ Today I am grateful for my ability to enjoy the morning sun and fresh air.
- ➢ I enjoy being with my friends and having good laughs.
- ➢ I am taking time to focus on other aspects of my life.
- ➢ I know that I am healing every moment.
- ➢ I'm giving my body all the time it needs.
- ➢ I am taking very good care of my body, mind, and spirit.
- ➢ I am doing everything possible to promote my full recovery.
- ➢ I am recovering like a true champion.

Part
V

Obstacles
as
Vehicles for
Healing

Chapter
18

Listening to the Wisdom of the Body

Learn to hear the whispers of the body and mind before they have to shout

An athlete came into my office complaining, "Whenever an important race comes up, something goes wrong, either mentally or physically. I can't seem to pull it all together when it really counts. I seem to be counterproductive, self-defeating, and continually sabotaging myself." I hear this type of complaint from athletes across the board, regardless of what sport or what level of play. For example, runners often fail to listen to their body's subtle messages, overtrain too close to their event, and wind up with an injury.

In team sports we're often taught by coaches not to pay too much attention to aches and pains. We're told: "Don't be a wimp – just get through the workout. We have a competition this Sunday." So we often ignore the subtle symptoms. We plod on, making sure we complete our designated weekly training, doing a small amount of tissue damage each day, until our body screams for attention. Once an injury sets in, the healing and recovery then take much longer than if we had learned to pay attention each day.

One of the most extraordinary examples of accelerated healing was Joan Benoit Samuelson's swift journey from hospital bed to victory stand. Only 17 days after having knee surgery, Joan recovered in record time and won the Olympic marathon trials, in 1984. She went on to win the Gold Medal in the first-ever women's Olympic marathon. A few years later I was asked to give a presentation on sports psychology at a running camp with Joan Benoit Samuelson and Bill Rodgers. During an early morning run with Joan, she related to me how visualizing healing and believing in herself made all the difference in her rapid recovery.

Sports Car Mentality

The body, in fact, has critical information for us. We need only to listen carefully, sense its soft messages, and follow its direction regularly. We need to first check in with our bodies before blindly moving ahead with our training plan. Indeed, to train consistently and to stay healthy, we need to treat and care for our bodies like a finely tuned sports car.

I worked with the athlete described above over a three-month period. I showed him a technique involving listening and dialoguing in which he learned to tune in to his body and mind with a sense of compassion and curiosity. In fact, he launched into a journey that led to profound and lasting change in his running, which then carried over to the rest of his life. I have used this dialoguing technique successfully with so many athletes that it is well worth incorporating into your training plans. The process does not take extra time, only a greater awareness during the time you are training.

What I'm proposing here is a body-oriented process of awareness and healing. You can learn a method of sensing how you feel – physically and mentally. Then you can have a dialogue with your feelings and sensations where you do most of the listening. Athletes tend to be action-oriented, driven, and goal-directed. They are accustomed to actively telling their bodies what to do - most of the time not so tactfully.

You may say to yourself: "Pick up the pace, you slug, your shoulders are too stiff, why aren't you catching that guy in front of you?" What do you do when an uncomfortable feeling develops in your body (e.g., your calf cramping or knee aching)? The typical reaction is to try to over-ride it. Perhaps you yell at it a bit: "Why does this stupid pain have to come on right now, when I've got 13 miles to go in the marathon?" Or you might beat yourself up mentally: "If only I had trained harder, my knee wouldn't freeze up like this."

Becoming Quiet and Listening

What does not occur to most athletes is to become quiet and to listen to the body's sensations. The key to preventing injury is to let your body give you this crucial feedback, especially while warming up for your regular workouts. Then you can take in and respect its wisdom before deciding on your course of action.

When you let the body speak, you are allowing yourself to be open to the depth and richness of your whole self – body, mind, and spirit. Once you pay attention to a sensation (e.g., tension or pain), it is more likely to release and let you go on with your training in a more clear and focused way. You'll also gain a better sense of what you need to do, if anything, to help the body function more efficiently (e.g., alter your posture, training form, breathing, etc.). Often we don't need to change anything at all. The body can heal and correct itself. Awareness alone can often take care of the problem.

Have you ever wondered during workout, "Am I doing the right thing for my body today? Should I be going this far or this fast when I'm just returning from an injury? Is this workout helping to strengthen that area, or is it further aggravating the tendons that are still weak and vulnerable? Am I ready to take my training to the next level, or should I be conservative and stay with the same workouts for another week?" Regular listening and dialoguing with the body, as I will describe below, can fully answer all these questions and give you a strong sense that you are doing the right thing.

Consulting With Your Body

It is now well accepted that we can confer with our bodies to decide if we are eating the proper food and if we are getting enough sleep. We understand that our bodies know what it feels like to be in good health, and what it's like when we're on the edge of a cold or flu or injury. We know the positive sensations of having energy to spare and being very focused. We also know when we've let ourselves become too tired or let our bodies become torn down.

Indeed, we understand how to recognize the extreme states, but what about the subtle stages in between? With demanding workouts that challenge the muscles and tissues to work harder, we are continually tearing the body down. And don't forget, the mind is also challenged and needs recovery. This repair and healing process is going on constantly, for both the body and mind. The question is what are you doing to be more aware and to facilitate the healing process?

Our bodies are wise in many ways beyond what is acknowledged by the average person. They can show us the path to optimal health and fitness if we so choose. Our bodies carry knowledge not only about how we are training, but how we are treating ourselves, what we value and believe, how we have been hurt emotionally, and how we are living our lives. Have you ever noticed when you think about that coach or parent who mistreated you, the pain in your neck or shoulder gets worse? Our bodies know which people are good for us to train with and which ones deplete and degrade us. And our physical selves know the best path to move up to the next level in our performance.

Below I have described an exercise for tuning in and listening to the body in a caring, non-judgmental way that can save you months of time being on the injured list. Using this technique of listening and dialoguing can become a window into this expansive domain of knowledge that is accessible through the body. This type of work allows you to hear the soft warnings of the body and mind before they have to scream for attention. Then you'll be on your way to remaining healthy throughout the year.

Benefits of Listening to the Body

What kinds of problems best lend themselves to this sort of technique?

➢ Athletes who are training hard but feel stuck can use this listening technique to get their training moving again. You may be wondering: "I keep doing the same workouts, but the progress isn't there. There's something I'm not understanding about my body and my training."

➢ Some athletes may need to work on addiction problems (e.g., overeating, drinking, drugs, or caffeine). This technique can help release you from the power of your addiction by allowing you to listen carefully to the part of you that is responsible for the addictive behavior, and gain its cooperation.

➢ Athletes who have difficult or overwhelming feelings can learn to have a better relationship with their emotions. Strong feelings (anger, fear, sadness) can sometimes wash over us like ocean waves, and they can interrupt effective training. However, these emotions are there for a reason. They have an important message to convey. They bring back an important part of our wholeness. We need to learn to listen to their story without becoming overwhelmed. With this technique, you can begin to have a comfortable relationship with strong feelings, and acknowledge them without being drowned by them.

➢ Competitive athletes often have a highly critical side that makes training less enjoyable. You may want to quiet your critical side and enhance self-acceptance. With practice, you can turn your inner critic into an ally and supporter. Once you accept all parts of yourself (e.g., even the part that sometimes gets injured), this will allow deeper and more meaningful improvement in your training.

Creating an Atmosphere of Trust

Before beginning the work of listening to the body, you need to first establish a safe, trusting environment for communication. Imagine for a moment that you are walking along a trail, and you notice a small bashful animal peeking out from behind a tree. The animal is not a danger to you, but you would like to help it feel safe and relaxed around you. How would you accomplish this? What atmosphere would you like to create? You certainly would not run toward it shouting. You would probably be still and patient, or move very slowly and gently. You would be interested in it, watching carefully for signs that it feels comfortable around you. You would notice when it might be all right to move in a little closer.

The technique of dialoguing with your body described below is a process of listening to something inside yourself that wants to communicate with you. Just like getting to know the shy animal, your body may first need to establish that you are trustworthy, that you have created a safe place for it to deliver its message. So you need to create a safe, non-judgmental environment to do this work.

The body's solutions are infinitely better, more creative, and healthier than anything your logical mind can dream up. You may feel stuck, but your body isn't. Once you begin to listen, understand, and dialogue with your body, it will show you its ageless wisdom. It will let you in on its critical secrets for staying healthy and moving forward with your training. You can then train more consistently and remain healthy throughout the year. You'll gain a new level of sensitivity to the body that can take you to new performance highs.

Awareness Exercise #1: Being in touch with your Body

Take a moment and notice what you are feeling right now in your body or mind. If you are working out, notice if you have any nagging pain. Is it possible to simply let the feeling be there without trying to change it? Just notice how you are in this moment and say: "Yes, this is how I feel." Or say to the uncomfortable sensation: "Yes, I know you're there." You may have a tendency to judge your body as soon as you notice any discomfort and say, "I shouldn't be feeling this way." Or you may try to analyze your body pain saying: "Why do I always feel this way? Why doesn't my body perform like I want it to?" None of these ways is effective in helping the situation. This usually creates more body tension and discomfort.

However, when you allow your bodily sensations to be as they are and just acknowledge them, then they can change for the better on their own. When they are allowed just to be, they can settle down to have a conversation with you, and that conversation leads to positive change. You can really tune in and understand what your symptoms are telling you.

I utilized this exercise with one of my athlete clients who was experiencing hamstring pain while training for an ice dancing competition. After acknowledging the sensation, she noticed an immediate sense of physical relief. She said: "The sensation is still there, but it's no longer painful. Now that it has my attention, it doesn't need to hurt and nag at me anymore."

Awareness Exercise #2: Dialoguing with your Body

Once you've established an area of your body that you would like to work on, you can begin a dialogue. Ask yourself: "What bodily sensation am I most aware of? What part needs my attention?" Once you identify a certain area, then ask yourself: "What exactly does it feel like?" Find the right words to describe it. Make sure you have the best words to fully articulate how it feels (e.g., tight shoulders, heavy feet, racing mind, etc.). You can write these thoughts down in a journal later.

Next, gently acknowledge its presence. You could say, for instance: "Yes, I know you're there." Rather than fighting with the body as we often do, saying, "Oh God, there's that darn knee pain again," this time you can simply notice the sensation with a quiet curiosity and begin to learn about it. Then just notice what happens. Become aware of any change in the sensation.

Now you can begin asking that part of the body what it needs. Or you can ask: "What needs to happen next for it to get better?" You can learn, for instance, if it just needs your quiet company? Does it need more care and attention? Does it need some special treatment?

Next you could ask your body to show you how "completely healed" would feel. How would it feel to have the problem cleared up, resolved satisfactorily? It's important to also listen to the "good" side of your body as well (e.g., check in with the other healthy knee to remind yourself of what that body part feels like when it is functioning well).

The body knows now how it would feel to have the situation resolved, even though your analytical mind may have no idea how that could happen. Ask your body to show you by beginning to feel that way right now. That kind of suggestion helps create an opening for new ways of being and perhaps healthier ways of treating your body.

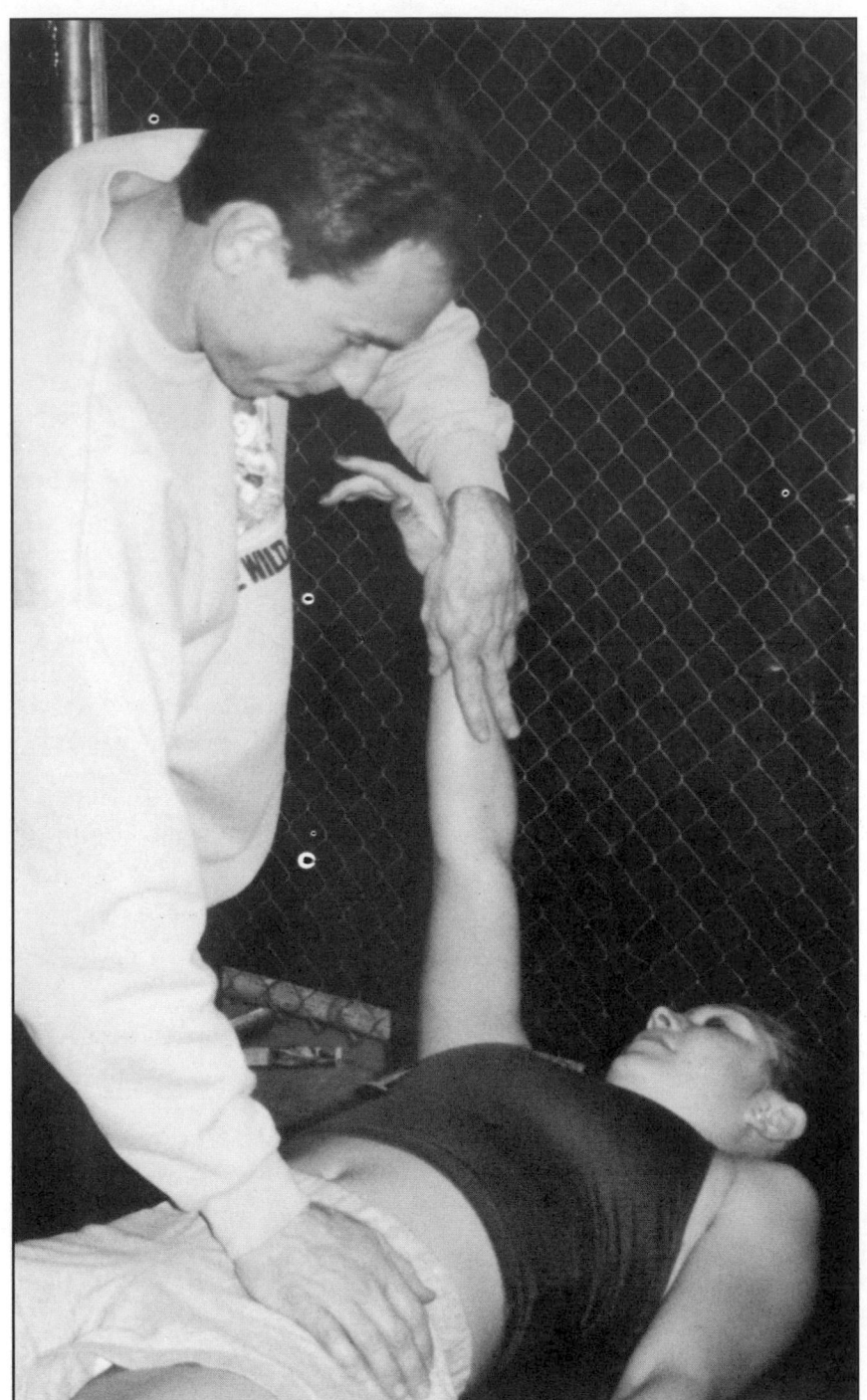

Chapter
19

Healing Mental
and
Physical Wounds

*The ability to
heal yourself is
probably the most
powerful skill
you will use
throughout your
lifetime*

The process of healing is complex, with many critical steps along the path to optimal health. You might view it as an adventure, a personal journey of self-discovery-- an opportunity to learn who you really are. Before the healing process can begin, you must confront several difficult issues. Emotional wounds need to be dealt with along with the physical pain. An injury is nature's way of getting your attention. The body is saying: "Hey, stop and listen, something is not right! Take a break, re-assess your training, and perhaps your life."

The cycles of growth and setback are inevitable, especially with the endurance sports of running, swimming, and biking. Athletes often attempt to fight these natural occurrences but find they are only delaying the healing process. In fact, becoming injured is a perfect opportunity for reflection about your life and your training.

Athletes go through several stages in their emotional response and adjustment to injury. You may have heard of Elizabeth Kubler-Ross's description of the five stages that most people go through in response to any major loss in their lives. Athletes, however, have particular needs in response to their loss of activity. In my clinical work with athletes over the years I have compiled a set of stages that most athletes progress through while moving from injury into health.

The seven stages of healing include: 1) Denial, 2) Bottoming Out, 3) Regret, 4) Despair, 5) Resistance, 6) Acceptance, and 7) Healing. Individuals may alternate back and forth through the different phases on their journey back to health. I have outlined each of these stages below by describing what happened with one of my athlete clients who had an overuse injury.

One Athlete's Story

Imagine the following scenario. Let's say you're a runner and you've got this important race on the horizon. You are committed to performing well, no matter what the cost.

Stage 1 – Denial: First you notice that something in your body feels a little funny (e.g., foot, leg, knee). You say to yourself, "It's not a big deal; I can train through this. I won't be a wimp." You continue your training, refusing to admit that this may be a serious problem.

However, after a few weeks, more activities seem to aggravate the problem. With each day you discover more things that you cannot do. First, you may try to cut back on your running, but the pain is still there. You try running on soft surfaces. This change helps a little, but you know that you're still not solving the problem.

You try new shoes, different orthotics, icing, Ibuprofen, massage, all the usual treatments. You begin cross-training on alternate days, which helps initially. But now you start to notice the pain even with walking after each run. You feel it getting in and out of the car. You sense it when you first get up in the morning. Then you notice that other areas of your body are starting to hurt. Without realizing it, you're starting to run in a slightly different way to manage the pain and weakness on one side. Compensation injuries start to set in on the opposite side of the body. Now you've got two sore spots.

You ask yourself, what is going on with me? I'm spending all my time just trying to recover for the next workout. I'm limping around like a disabled person and icing all day. Your friends are asking, are you sure you should be running when you can't even walk right? But you tell yourself, I'm in such great shape with all this training, I can't give up now. I'm really healthy, right? This race means so much to me. That little voice inside tries so hard to give you its important message, but as with a drug addict, the denial sets in even deeper. You put your head down and keep on training even though your body is crying out for rest - lots of rest.

Now the race is only three weeks away and you begin to get really scared. You're thinking, "God, am I doing serious damage to my body? There's got to be a way out of this. If there's a wonder drug, I'll take anything just to get to the finish line." Out of desperation, you finally decide to go to your podiatrist and ask for a cortisone shot. You say to yourself: "OK, this is only short-term. I'm just getting this injection to reduce the inflammation. I'm not doing it just to cover up the pain." The shot, in fact, does help you through the next two runs. It's like a miracle cure, for a short period. But, of course, the effects wear off in the next few days, and you're back to square one. Like an addict, you are thinking, "I wonder if another cortisone shot - a stronger one - would help even more? I'll get one right before the race, and I won't feel a thing. I'll breeze through the race, no problem. I'll deal with the effects later."

The week before your big race, anxiety continues to build. A third compensation injury begins to set in because of running incorrectly. Not only do you have the normal tension before an important race, you have another layer of anxiety that is far greater, associated with all the accumulating injuries. The questions keep coming up. "What am I doing to myself? I can't even walk or drive without pain. How am I going to run this entire race?" The feelings of obligation set in. You become blinded by your goal. "I've told all my friends and family that I'm going to complete this thing. I can't let them down. This may be my last chance to ever meet this important goal. People are depending on me to finish. I know I've got to go through with this no matter what. Once I set a goal, there's no altering it." The black and white thinking takes over.

Of course, you attempt the race, and the body doesn't hold up. You feel the pain right from the first mile of the race. You do even more bodily damage and end up having to drop out. You feel devastated after 6 months of hard work. The week afterward, you have to deal with all the questions: "Well, how did it go?" You have the chore of telling what feels like a million people that you didn't come through with your goal. The one question you forgot to ask yourself during this whole process is: "What will my life look like after this race, if my body doesn't hold up?"

The agony of injury turns the athlete's world upside down. During this time the injured athlete is actually undergoing a crisis. In addition to the physical wound, tension, fear, anxiety, depression, and even panic can appear. These emotional responses create even more stress that exacerbates the existing pain.

Stage 2 - Bottoming Out: Let's continue with our scenario into the second stage. Once you're injured and finally decide to take time off training, something shifts on a very deep level inside you. You begin to look at the world differently. At first you feel numb. You have a sense of not caring about anything or anyone. With inactivity, the boredom sets in. Everything seems more dismal and desolate. You can lose perspective on your goals and priorities. You may wallow in self-pity. You feel out of control, as if there's nothing you can do about your situation. You feel that your body has betrayed you. The injured part becomes your enemy rather than your friend.

Stage 3 – Regret: After a few more days, reality sets in. The consequences of your over-training become more apparent. The denial wears off, just like the effects of a drug. After not running for a short while, you begin to experience the strong negative feelings of withdrawal from your daily endorphin fix. You experience irritability, self-doubt, impatience, and anxiety.

The questions just keep coming. What have I done to myself? How could I be so blind? Why didn't I see the warning signs? Why didn't I listen to what people were telling me? You start beating yourself up mentally. You say, I'm a fairly intelligent person. How could I not see this coming? How could I get so wrapped up in this goal that I left my body's needs behind? You realize how much of your life you gave up in pursuit of this objective. You say: "If only I would have..., could have..., I would have done things much differently." The mountain of regret – it will eat you up inside if you stay in it. After you've exhausted all the things and people you can blame for your injury (e.g., the incorrect shoes, bad coaching), you find the only one left to confront is yourself.

Stage 4 – Despair, Assessing the Damage: After the first week of numbness stemming from the whole event, you begin to evaluate what you've done to your body. You find out just how much damage was done. At first you might think, "Oh, it's not that bad. I'll just take a week off running. Then I'll be healed and ready to go." As things start to feel better, of course, you start doing more. You may find out that, in fact, you are only five percent better. You then notice that even gentle walking aggravates the problem. You find out just how limited you are, at least for a while. You realize how much you cannot do. Of course, running is out of the question for a while, maybe longer than you initially thought. But now you realize that bicycling hurts as well. All your favorite activities are off the list. Depression can easily set in at this point. Mood changes can also bring on other self-destructive habits, such as overeating or increased alcohol use.

Stage 5 - Resistance to Change: When you can't participate in one activity, the natural instinct is to move on to an alternative activity with even more enthusiasm. You might try swimming. The problem is you're using new muscles that quickly get overloaded. Swimming might work well for a few days, until you bring on a major shoulder injury from too much of a good thing. Now you find out how many activities hurt when you use your arms. Your shoulder cries out, especially when you use your computer at work. So your work productivity goes downhill fast.

The activity has changed, but the high stress mental gear that brought the problem on initially has remained the same. So now you've got several compensation injuries. At some point, the multiple aches and pains become so overwhelming that surrender and rest are the only option. That's when the real healing begins.

Stage 6 - Acceptance - The Way Out: Athletes often fight their recovery and inadvertently sabotage the healing process. Athletes are so used to a fast-paced lifestyle that they forget how to use the other available gears. This ongoing stress can weaken the immune system and prolong the healing of injuries. Slowing down and resting is so contrary to the mindset of the over-achiever. Yet once we do slow down, we can really see and hear clearly what is going on within our bodies. We gain a sense of intimacy with ourselves. Once we put some time and space around us, we can change our relationship with the pain or injury. We can be with it differently. We can move into a new phase of acceptance.

Acceptance is simply learning to be with what is and allowing it to be all right. It is being completely aware of what is happening in this moment and not fighting it. You accept everything as it arises with neutrality and respect. Acceptance is being mindful of the stage you are in right now, without judgment or criticism. You surrender to the injury and forgive yourself for everything leading up to it. Once you fully accept that you are injured, you can also acknowledge that you are fully capable of healing.

Stage 7 - Healing - Turning It Around: Once you truly accept that you're injured, you'll notice a shift deep inside, and you can begin the healing process. Injury is nature's way of telling you that you deserve a rest. The body has an amazing ability to heal itself once you allow it to do its job. The body wants to heal and be whole again; it wants to move toward balance and perfection. But your anxiety and worry often prevent that process from moving forward. For optimal healing, you need to get your mind out of the way to let the body do the work of healing. You can take this opportunity to re-evaluate your life and find a new, more healthy equilibrium.

Learning About Your Injury

As athletes, we often train ourselves to block out pain sensations, to continue training regardless of what the body is saying. However, in recovering from an injury, just the opposite needs to happen. Here are some suggestions:

➢ Learn as much as you can about what's going on in your body and what it needs to recover. Take on an attitude of quiet observation, of curiosity, without being critical or judgmental. Be gentle with yourself. Develop a sense of relaxed attention.

➢ Do your own personal investigation. Become mindful of every movement throughout each day. Note what aggravates the injury and what activities you need to avoid.

➢ Take an active role in your recovery. Make a list of all the things you need to be doing to promote the healing process (e.g., stretching, icing, visualization). Place it in plain view, wherever you are (e.g., use post-its or messages on your computer).

➢ Draw out the positive lessons from your injury so you can avoid repeating the same mistakes when you return to training. Continue to gather wisdom from your experience to promote lifelong learning.

Facilitating the Healing Process

Keeping a positive attitude and remaining motivated are critical components of complete healing. The body has an incredible ability to heal itself once you provide the right environment. I have seen powerful examples of healing in my clients when they give their body a steady diet of positive energy. When your mind is in the right place, the body will follow. You can utilize the same determination and tenacity for creating healing that you do for competing in a race. Here are some powerful tools for facilitating healing:

Switching Gears: Injury is a time to move from a fast-paced racing mode into a quiet time of rest, relaxation, and rejuvenation. Observe and accept your condition. Don't force your recovery. Be patient and allow it to happen. When you learn to relax more fully, you increase blood flow to injured areas and improve circulation, which can accelerate healing. Remove the pressure, throw away the race deadlines, and trust your body to heal in its own time frame. Your recovery process will then be enhanced.

Creating Images: The mind-body connection is so powerful you can actually control your capacity to heal. By imagining the healing process, you can direct your body to heal more efficiently. Use specific imagery to visualize the injured area being nurtured, strengthened, and healed. Then do more general imagery to see and feel yourself as peaceful, healthy, active, and in good spirits. Experience yourself doing the activities you'd like to be doing and feeling the way you want to feel. See yourself moving freely, performing well, and having fun.

Building a Positive Attitude: Believe in your continued capacity to heal yourself. Hold on to your vision of becoming fully healthy again. Don't let negative thoughts or other people get in your way. Focus on what you can do, not what you can't. Remember that progress always comes in cycles. There may be steps forward followed by small setbacks. Keep track of your progress, even the tiniest movement forward. Allow your dreams to guide you past the obstacles on the path toward full recovery.

Re-directing Your Attention: Take the energy you used for training and refocus it into active healing. Instead of setting race targets, develop goals directed toward health. Commit yourself to following your rehabilitation program. Then get involved in a project, something creative you've always wanted to do. Replace the intensity of training with something just as fascinating to hold your attention (e.g., start that book you've always wanted to write).

Stay Connected: Find other people who are injured and talk to them about their experiences. Don't dwell on the contrasts with others; focus on the similarities in your situations. Realize that many people have gone through similar suffering with their injuries. Remember Lance Armstrong, who progressed from having cancer, with only a 50% chance of living, to winning the Tour de France in 1999 and repeating in 2000. If he can do it, what is holding you back? Attitude is what makes the difference. Build a sense of connectedness. Find a recovery buddy and encourage each other in your healing journey.

Lessons to Be Learned

The greatest learning goes on during life's most challenging struggles. When we go to a place of deep soul searching, we acquire tremendous knowledge about what we are made of. Here are some critical lessons you can acquire through the healing process:

➢ Every wound has its wisdom. Find out what yours is telling you.

➢ Listen to that little voice inside when it quietly begins to call.

➢ Be cautious; you've only got one body, treat it right.

➢ Be happy with what you do have; work with what you can do.

➢ Learn to be less rigid in your thinking and planning.

➢ Gain knowledge about handling adversity and resilience.

➢ Become wiser and avoid the problem of coming back too soon.

➢ Use imagery to enhance any therapy you are undergoing. Your medical treatment comes from the outside, healing comes from within.

➢ Pay attention to your limits and move up to them slowly. Your body will learn how to move in a healthy manner over time.

➢ Choose your path carefully. When you're injured, you are in a crisis - the Chinese word for crisis is danger/opportunity.

➢ Appreciate that there is a lesson in everything that occurs in life.

➢ Trust and respect your body's wisdom. You will arrive at a new equilibrium, a new balance and a better level of functioning.

The path toward healing will eventually take you to a higher level in your character strength and wisdom. Accept that you will heal; trust and respect your body's wisdom. Look for reasons to believe in yourself and your ability to heal. Keep your vision in front of you, and you can pull through any hardship. Healing teaches the discipline of patience.

Visualization Exercise: Healing Your Injury

In this exercise you'll learn to visualize the physical healing process, and you'll work with any treatment method you may be undergoing. You'll then use creative images to represent your injury and its healing, and you'll project a healthy image into your future.

Sit or lie down in a comfortable position and close your eyes. Relax and begin to focus on your injury as if you were looking at it under a microscope. Visualize healthy tissue being built up like the Great Pyramid, or tender shoots growing into vibrant plants. Imagine you're laying new skin cells like tiles on a floor or kneading damaged muscle fibers like bread dough to improve flexibility. You could imagine white blood cells picking up the broken bones and building bridges between them. See the healthy cells around your injury multiplying, nuclei separating and dividing. See this happening all around your injury, filling in the missing pieces, and making your whole body uniform and strong again. Imagine blood vessels carrying oxygen and nutrients to your cells.

Imagine the treatment you are receiving. If you are doing rehabilitation, notice how exercise is stimulating the growth of new cells. Create a network of tendons and nerve fibers like interlaced branches, and see how each exercise is making your neural messages and soft tissue movement stronger and more precise. Watch your medication (if any) having the exact effect you want in your body.

Continue this process by bringing in other representations of your injury and the healing process. You can go beyond the physical tissue imagery, using objects, colors, lights, sounds, etc. If you have a strained calf muscle, see it as pulled out of shape. Then give yourself a pair of sculptor's hands, and mold the muscle back into its perfect position. Or visualize a golden ball of healing energy circling and warming the injured area.

Finally, finish your session with a vision of the future. See a picture of you taking the best possible care of yourself, eating well, exercising regularly, getting good sleep, and going to your doctor or physical therapy. Notice that you are gradually doing more and more, feeling better, coping with stress well, and having enough time and energy for all that you need to accomplish. Eventually, see yourself as completely healed, getting back into training, and returning to your previous fitness level and beyond.

Chapter
20

Managing
Difficult Emotions:
Sailing through
the Seasons

*When the heart
is nourished
through the senses,
the body moves
with ease*

Spring is a time for new beginnings and moving forward with our lives. It is a time when many athletes regain their energy and motivation to train. They set new goals and make specific plans for personal improvement in the new season.

Winter, in contrast, appears to be a difficult season for many individuals to endure, athletes included. During the long winter months, we notice the shorter days, with cold, stormy weather, and darkness in the sky that can seem to last forever. This inevitably creates havoc with an athlete's training schedule and motivation. In my practice I generally see a sharp increase in the number of depressed or anxious clients, due in large part to the change of seasons. More athletes report that their energy level drops and their inclination to train begins to wane.

Consider the fact that 16 million Americans suffer what is known as Seasonal Affective Disorder (SAD), also called Winter Depression. This condition seems to be brought on by the winter season and generally subsides in the springtime. The essential feature of this diagnosis is either a depressed mood or a loss of interest in most daily activities, including sports.

Classic Symptoms of Winter Depression:

➤ **Depressed mood most of the day:** Feeling sad, hopeless, discouraged, or not caring - having no feelings

➤ **Loss of interest or pleasure:** Less interest in activities that were previously pleasurable (e.g., exercising), social withdrawal, reduction in sexual interest

➤ **Change in appetite:** Increased caloric intake, craving of specific foods (sweets or fats), or reduced desire for food when severely depressed, with swings in body weight

➤ **Sleep disturbance:** Trouble going to sleep, staying asleep, or oversleeping (increased daytime sleep; difficulty getting out of bed)

➤ **Agitation:** Irritability, restlessness, inability to sit still

➤ **Fatigue or loss of energy:** Tiredness or low energy even with no exertion, athletic training seeming much harder than usual

➤ **Feelings of worthlessness or guilt:** Unrealistic negative evaluations of one's self worth, rumination on past failings, a pre-occupation with self-blame, an exaggerated sense of responsibility for events beyond one's control (e.g., an athlete being overcritical of past race results or injuries)

➤ **Impaired ability to concentrate:** Difficulty focusing and trouble making decisions, memory problems (e.g., becoming easily distracted during workouts)

Spring's Awakening

With the advent of spring, just like bears coming out of hibernation, we seem to re-awaken on many levels. We notice the longer days, more sunshine, flowers blossoming, birds singing, new trails to explore, and athletes from every sport coming out to train. In spring many of the symptoms named above seem to naturally reverse themselves. People begin to notice their moods lifting, an enhanced interest in most activities – especially training. The clients in my office generally feel more energy and are better able to focus. They start eating more healthfully, sleep more soundly, feel a higher sense of self-esteem, and are more excited about life. In fact during spring, they are less likely to seek treatment for depression, but are now in need of consultation on how to train mentally and physically, and get into peak shape for summer.

The Effect of Light

Why is Seasonal Affective Disorder so prevalent in the winter and so infrequent in the springtime? Our visual system is both an image processing unit and a light meter for the brain and body. Humans are indeed "solar powered." Since light affects the hormonal system, it impacts every cell in the body. We can think of light as "natural Prozac," as it optimizes levels of key neurotransmitters and hormones, such as seratonin, norepinephrine, and melatonin, which stabilize mood and mental activity. This in turn certainly enhances both our mental and physical energy level while increasing our motivation to train and perform better.

Today a large percentage of our time is spent indoors under light that is inadequate for our biological and psychological needs. Our bodies and minds are crying out for more light. Spring delivers that needed light just in time.

The effect of light is so powerful that people have begun using "light therapy" to help with symptoms of Seasonal Affective Disorder during winter. Individuals with SAD have seen positive results within days by spending between one and two hours per day in front of a specially designed "bright light box" or lamp that gives off at least 10,000 LUX units of light. The intensity level is about equal to a typical sun lamp. This type of light therapy has been used to maximize the performance of NASA astronauts during fifteen different space shuttle missions. Some athletes are now also using this method to improve their performance during the winter months.

Using Spring to Your Advantage

So what can you do to let spring bring out the best in you?

➢ Become an early riser – Get up early and soak up energy from the morning sun; go to bed earlier when the sun is no longer powering your body's solar panels.

➢ Get more light – Go for a walk at noontime during peak sunlight hours to take in more of that natural Prozac, and provide your body with vitamin D.

➢ Use your energy wisely - Go for your workout during the time of day when you have the most energy and motivation.

➢ Plan your spring training program – Set challenging yet realistic goals; avoid getting overly excited by doing too many races, leading to possible injury.

➢ Enjoy the longer days –Try some evening twilight workouts to experience some inspiring sunsets.

➢ Open up your senses – Take time to smell the blossoming wildflowers, hear the birds singing, feel the freshness in the air, and see the sky changing colors.

➢ Take advantage of the drier terrain – Get in awesome shape by doing more scenic hilly trail workouts; explore new routes you've never seen before.

➢ Improve your social life – Join an athletic club, participate in group workouts, go early and leave late, allowing time to connect with people and enjoy your endorphin highs together.

➢ Improve your Eating Habits – Cut down on caffeine to improve your sleep, eat more of the fresh fruits of spring, drink more water and juice to re-hydrate, and watch your body take on a fantastic shape.

➢ Try out new sports – If you're a runner, try cycling or swimming for cross training; if you play tennis, try skating or experiment with a new activity you've never done before, just for fun.

> "The changing seasons provide a context to change daily patterns and set new priorities," says Jonathan Beverly, Editor of *Running Times Magazine*. "After a summer of sun, heat and long days, I look forward to the romance of cold, dark evenings with stars blazing above snow-covered fields. I welcome the biting wind of autumn as heartily as the first warm breeze of spring. Every season, no matter how perfect, would grow stale if it continued unabated throughout the year."

Spring is a time to re-awaken our senses and recharge our batteries. It's also a great time to renew our commitment to achieving excellent health and fitness. So soak up the excitement and freshness in the air. Spend more time outside doing exactly what you want to be doing, and enjoy the energy of spring.

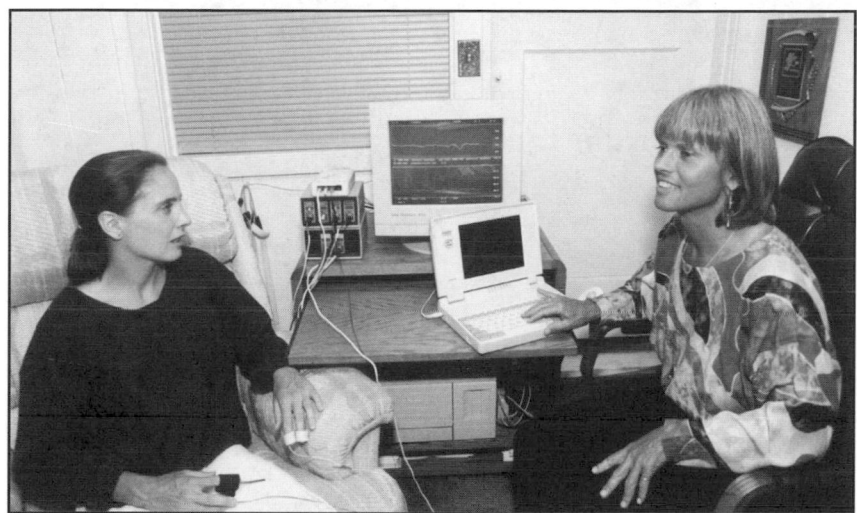

© Geoffrey Faraghan

Visualization for Spring

Relax your body and mind; begin to tune into your senses. As you breathe slowly and deeply, imagine doing one of your favorite morning workouts in early spring. Bring all five senses to life. Notice how your body is moving; check in with how you are feeling; connect your inner and outer world.

Begin to nourish your body and spirit through the senses. Take time to smell the freshness in the air; let your eyes picture a colorful carpet of wildflowers. Watch a butterfly fluttering on an iris. Notice your state of mind, your level of awareness, and your energy. Open up your heart and take in everything around you like a sponge. Once you recognize the beauty all around, you can embrace it and feel an inner strength and value within yourself.

Learn to begin each day with this kind of appreciation. Enter each workout with a sense of gratitude for every moment of your existence.

Chapter
21

Active Women:
Body Image
and Weight Issues

*Make your body
a partner in
your quest for
ultimate health*

Beauty and physical fitness are primary goals for many women in today's society. Body image, weight management, and eating problems have joined sex as the central issues in the lives of women. Athletes are no exception to this rule. Virtually every woman's magazine has a diet column. Diet clinics and medications are prevalent in the media and on the internet. The brand names of low-fat, low-sugar, and low-salt foods are part of our general vocabulary. This preoccupation with food, fat, and looking good has become a predominant concern in American society. Becoming obsessed with weight and the compulsion to overeat and diet are, in fact, serious and distressing experiences for many women athletes. This fact is confirmed by the growing number of women athletes with eating disorders.

Where does this obsession with body image come from? The importance of presentation as the central aspect of a woman's existence makes her tremendously self-conscious. For men in our society, power, status, and money are greatly emphasized; for women, it's our appearance. Men gaze at women. Women watch themselves being looked at. The way a woman is viewed by others most often determines the relationship she has with herself. The next time you go to a competition, spend a few minutes afterward observing how much "checking out" is going on, and how many conversations revolve around body image and thinness (e.g., "can you believe how much weight that woman has gained since she was injured in that last race?").

Appearance as a Commodity

The emphasis on appearance demands that a woman preoccupy herself with obtaining an image that others will find attractive and pleasing. This outer image becomes the symbol for who she is as a woman. She is expected to examine and scrutinize every aspect of herself as though she were constantly being judged. She learns about the proper image of womanhood from TV ads, billboards, magazines, and the internet. The media present women in one of two prescribed roles, either in the sexual context or within the family, as a wife or mother. To attract someone, she must look appealing, sensual, innocent, mysterious, and above all, thin. For athletes, appearing physically fit is a significant part of this picture. Women usually begin exercising for the purpose of losing weight and looking better, rather than for inner satisfaction and health.

Since women are taught to view themselves from the outside, they fall prey to the enormous fashion and weight reduction industries. These companies first establish an ideal body image and then pressure women into meeting that standard. The message being communicated is that a woman's body is not acceptable as it is. It must be fit, thin, well-groomed, perfumed, and tastefully clothed. It must measure up to an ideal physical type. Of course, this task is never-ending, because the ideal body image changes over the years. As clothes styles change seasonally, women's bodies are expected to shift in order to fit these fashions – tall and daring one year, petite and modest the next.

Coaches often inadvertently push this ideal body image onto their female athletes (e.g., "if you could gain some self-control and lose a few more pounds, you could move a lot faster, and help the team out even more!"). So women quickly make the mental connection: Restrict calories = lose weight = win the race!

Women athletes are continually manipulated by images of "proper femininity," which are extremely powerful because they are presented as the only reality. Women are encouraged to conform or run the risk of being outcast. Thus, they are caught up in an attempt to match a standard that is externally defined and continually changing. These representations of femininity are experienced by most women as frightening and unattainable. They produce a picture that is far from the reality of women's day-to-day lives.

Thinking Differently about the Body

So how can women learn to deal more constructively with these societal pressures and nurture themselves in positive ways? Clearly women need to address the issue of self-image. In my practice, I advise my female clients to start placing the emphasis on intrinsic qualities, not on external appearance. They need to be less concerned about the evaluations of others and focus on internal acceptance of themselves, regardless of body size or shape. The greater one's inner strength and self-esteem, the less need there is to gain someone else's approval.

Body Intelligence

Here are two exercises you can do to assess how much you know about your own body and what it needs. Women focus a great deal of attention on their bodies and how they look from the outside. Yet the body's appearance is only one aspect of the self.

Close your eyes, take 10 deep breaths, and ask yourself these questions. Then write down your responses, and notice any new insights you may have about yourself.

Part 1: Which part of your body:

Are you most comfortable with?
Do people notice first?
Is strongest?
Is most injury-prone?
Are you most self-conscious about?
Do you like the most?

Part 2: Pretend that you live outside your body and that someone else could move in. What tips would you give the new occupant about what it's like to be there?

1) What kind of care does it need?
   Attention, food, hydration, light, exercise, proper environment, social support, physical affection, healing, and recovery?
2) What are its rhythms or routines?
   Hourly, daily, weekly, monthly, seasonally?
3) What tips can you suggest for how to manage this body?
   Knowing when to stop working and provide adequate rest, knowing when to take an easy training day?
4) How do other people respond to this body?
   How much does that matter?

Juggling Multiple Roles

Now that you've completed these exercises, let's look deeper into why eating, weight management, and body image present various problems for women athletes. The roots of this dilemma may be found in the life transitions a woman experiences. Moving through many different roles throughout life can be challenging for most women, especially if they are physically active. Transitioning into the new roles of mate, spouse, and mother can often play havoc with a woman's self-esteem as well as her exercise program.

As spouses or mothers, women usually place everyone else's needs first. Mothers often take on the role of unpaid supervisors of small, vital, complex, and demanding organizations. Although the spouse may help, women are primarily responsible for the day-to-day operations. Each day they often work an estimated eight hours at home, plus eight extra hours at their job outside the home. They usually make sure the food is purchased and prepared, the house cleaned and comfortable, the laundry done, the children well managed, and toys put away. They chauffeur the kids to school and to their extra-curricular activities. They do the social-secretarial work of arranging for the family to spend time with friends and relatives. If the woman is a single mother, these tasks can be even more demanding.

Women often work full-time, constantly making sure that everyone else's life runs smoothly. Only then can they care for themselves and perhaps squeeze in an evening 20-minute run or bike. They are relentlessly giving, without receiving the credit that would validate their personal worth.

The one desirable goal that is constant in all these models, whether a woman is single, married, or a mother, is that of thinness. In attempting to conform to this image, women experience particular pressure around food and eating. Media preoccupation with good housekeeping and good eating habits serves as a measuring stick to constantly judge a woman's performance. The media present a long list of do's and don'ts about food choices that is contradictory and confusing. Whether she is breast-feeding her baby, trying to get her child to eat vegetables, or feeding herself after a hard workout, the woman is often made to feel inadequate about her ability to perform this fundamental task. No wonder women quickly learn not to trust their own impulses in nurturing themselves. They are constantly feeding the world and attending to the needs of others. As such, they are often confused about their own bodily needs.

One form of giving back and replenishing one's reserves is through food. In my practice I often hear women complain: "I take care of my spouse, my kids, my mother, and so many people that pass in and out of the house." "I feel so empty and drained with all of this giving that I eat to fill up the emotional void inside." "I am usually so wiped out that I don't have the energy to work out. My judgment goes out the window, and I make poor food choices." These kinds of statements represent the major struggle that goes on inside the minds of many women as they attempt to juggle their multiple roles of mate, mother, employer, and athlete.

Re-Defining Healthy Weight

So how can women athletes find greater satisfaction and a sense of well-being in the bodies that they have? How can they put an end to the obsessing about fat, food, and appearance? Women need to define healthy weight in a new way. Rather than looking at the doctor's height/weight chart, you can think of a healthy weight as the size your body naturally finds when you are living a reasonable life. It is that weight that your body moves toward when you are not obsessing about food, but rather living a balanced life of moderation in eating and exercising. For most women this weight may be a bit higher than they think it should be, since our culture promotes and reinforces only the leanest bodies. People come in all sizes and shapes, and many factors contribute to healthy weight, not only food intake.

Research has continually shown that dieting does not work. Most studies indicate that dieters cannot maintain weight loss for more than a few months. Instead we see evidence that each type of body utilizes fuel differently and that heredity plays a substantial role in the process of metabolism.

From my clinical work with people across the weight spectrum, it seems that we can't choose some arbitrary figure on the scale and turn our lives upside down to arrive there. Instead, there is probably some range of weight that your body settles into when you are living a normal, fulfilling life - when you're not eating, dieting, or exercising compulsively. You can't live an unhealthy life and arrive at a healthy weight – not one that will last.

Regardless of your size, if you are struggling with food, weight, or body image, the solution looks much the same. You need to let the weight issue move into the background and instead focus on self-esteem and quality of life. Rather than struggling with your body, make it a partner in your quest for ultimate health. Learn more about what your body needs and take good care of it. Nurture yourself in many different ways, not only through food. Fortify yourself to withstand society's negative messages about fat, femaleness, and failure. Become more interested in inner satisfaction and less focused on pleasing others through outward appearance.

© John Segesta – Triathlete Magazine

Tools for Awareness and Change

➤ Learn to fully appreciate the body that you have.

➤ Make only those personal changes you can live with in the long run.

➤ Exercise according to your body's needs, not just your training plan.

➤ Check in with your body before making choices about eating. Let it tell you when it's hungry or full. Learn to trust your body and its messages.

➤ View food as nourishment, not just as pleasure.

➤ Reward yourself in many ways, not only with unhealthy foods.

➤ Ask for what you need from your family and friends, but seek help elsewhere if they cannot provide it.

Katherine Switzer was the 1974 New York City Marathon Champion and is now TV commentator for the New York, Boston, and Los Angeles Marathons. She was a pioneer in securing the women's marathon as an Olympic event. Katherine feels that exercise is the key to developing a better body image. She says, "You will start liking and appreciating your body more once it's moving." To avoid feeling self-conscious about onlookers, she suggests: "Do Women's-Only events, and you won't have to worry about intimidation. If you move your body every day, you will become more self-confident, and eventually you won't care what other people think."

The challenge for women is to move away from obsessing about body image and weight loss and focus more on improving health and quality of life. It is important to get off the endless roller coaster of feeling fat, dieting, feeling deprived, overeating to fill the emotional void, feeling guilty, and then repeating the cycle. The key is body–competence: learning to fully accept the body you are given. Once you have a better relationship with yourself, you are more motivated to take good care of your body. You can be more in tune with its needs and discover a variety of ways to challenge, soothe, nourish, and rest your body. Then you can free your energy for engaging in the more exciting activities of life. You can work out for the right reasons, enjoy training to the fullest, and do it completely for yourself.

Try the following exercises once each day. Once you start to feel good about yourself from the inside, you'll project the same healthy energy outward. You won't have to worry about how you look. Your body will naturally radiate good health and fitness.

Body Appreciation: Exercise #1

Close your eyes, take five deep breaths, and ask yourself this question: What has my body done for me lately? Think about the wide range of possibilities. Then write down all of your responses. Perhaps your body has:

➤ Pulled through a fantastic workout
➤ Healed completely from an injury or illness
➤ Recovered well during sleep
➤ Allowed you to feel more enjoyment in life
➤ Become stronger and more flexible
➤ Learned a new skill
➤ Given you satisfaction by achieving an important goal
➤ Become more healthy, fit, and attractive
➤ Reached out and made new friends
➤ Allowed you to feel the nurturing touch of another person
➤ Given you sexual pleasure
➤ Created another human being
➤ Learned to relax mentally and physically

Body Appreciation: Exercise #2

Now, once again, close your eyes, relax, and breathe deeply. Picture the responses you have just written down in exercise #1. As these images come and go through your mind, become aware of any feelings that arise. You may notice positive feelings toward your body. Perhaps there is also anger or frustration. Just be with whatever feelings appear; experience them fully.

Now consider one thing that you appreciate about your body. It might be difficult, but just breathe, and accept whatever comes to mind. It may be a talent, an attribute, an accomplishment, or just a way of being. Now feel a sense of wonder and amazement about this gift from your body. What words capture the positive feeling you have for this gift? You may want to say them out loud. They may be words of kindness and appreciation that you could make time to say more often. From this day on remember to allow yourself a few moments each day to reflect and appreciate who you are and what your body has done for you.

Part VI

Finding Meaning
in
Your Pursuits

Chapter
22

Creating Balance
in Your Life

*Strive for
integration
so that each part
of your life
supports every other
part of your being*

A balanced lifestyle allows us to perform with enthusiasm and a sense of purpose, with the potential for remarkable accomplishments. Great athletes are able to manage lives that have diversity and balance. Loss and disappointment are easier to handle when you have other things in life to fall back on. In contrast, a life that is unbalanced is also unstable, and can take away from your quest toward achievement. Balance and excellence compliment one another in powerful ways.

A life without balance comes with a price. Even for those who do well, success rarely makes up for what one loses by being self-absorbed. The rest of one's life is put on hold for long periods of time. Friendships are often lost and family life suffers. This uneven existence reveals its consequences when the short-lived applause and awards are no longer satisfying.

> I interviewed Mark Allen, six-time winner of the Hawaii Ironman Triathlon and ten-time undefeated champion of the Nice International Triathlon World Championship. He looked back on his series of victories: "I had tried for six years to win in Hawaii, and each time I came up short. In 1989 I finally achieved my goal and won the Ironman. I said to myself, WOW! Then I won it again in 1990, and the WOW was not as great. I continued to win in '91, '92, and '93. Each time the WOW was a little less. The successes were not as fulfilling. I asked myself, how many of these do I have to win before it becomes a lasting feeling?"

To excel in their sport, athletes often become unbalanced in their approach to training. When you are focused on an upcoming competition, it may appear that you can never do enough to get ready. It can be tempting to train during every free moment that you have available. You can get behind in your work and neglect your family and friends in order to feed the compulsion to train. Eventually you realize that a lifestyle of extremes takes its toll emotionally and physically.

In my work with many athletes of all levels I have noticed that the ones who are well rounded tend to be far more successful and satisfied with their lives. They are also healthier and have more longevity in their sport. They distribute their time among a variety of activities, giving appropriate amounts of energy to work, family, and friends. They allocate time for creative endeavors, time for learning new skills, and time for pure fun. Most of all they allow quiet time for themselves to slow down and reflect, and to feel grateful for each day.

What Does Balance Mean?

I recently conducted a survey by asking a large number of my athlete clients what it meant to have balance in their lives. I received a variety of enlightened responses:

➢ "Balance is finding beauty, passion, and meaning in any activity."
➢ "Balance is being content with yourself, not tying your personal worth to the race results."
➢ "To have balance you need to engage in quality recovery time and take good care of yourself."
➢ "I am seasonally balanced. I am very focused during the competitive season, but then I really kick back in the winter."
➢ "Your highs are really high, your lows are really low, but with a balanced life at least you know where you're going."
➢ "Balance is being exactly where you want to be, doing what you want to do."
➢ "Balance is being in peak shape and walking that fine line between top form and injury."
➢ "When I'm around people who give me energy, I get my balance back."
➢ "I need other things to rely on in my life besides sports to feel balanced."

One of my athlete clients who trained obsessively said she learned about balance when a family member died during the peak competitive season. She discovered that there were far more important elements in life than just training. That event helped her to put things into perspective. She realized that family and friends are essential to her emotional health and that her life needed more balance.

In my professional work with athletes I have observed that those who are most successful and content have learned to balance their lives. They say that having a good relationship, a career, close friends, and leisure pursuits has allowed them to compete feeling more relaxed and secure. Athletes note that when they become too absorbed in their sport they tend to overanalyze and criticize their training. Every workout can take on monumental importance. When they have other life concerns to focus on, training takes on a more healthy perspective.

If your life is out of balance, nature has a way of getting your attention so that you re-establish it. Unfortunately sometimes the message can be quite painful, in the form of fatigue, an illness, an injury, or burnout. In the case of a high-stress lifestyle over many years, the message could be the development of cancer or a heart attack. Excessive attention to any one area of life – work, family, diet, alcohol, or exercise - can lead you down the road to personal ruin. Moderation is the path to creating balance.

The key to building a lifestyle of moderation is in knowing how much is enough. It is having a sense of when to stop an activity before it becomes self-destructive. It is the art of being conservative and sensible about your training, working, eating, and every other area of your life. For every period of intensity, we also need a time to back off and relax.

Athletes often have trouble with this concept of backing off early. Let's say you acquire a hamstring injury from the previous day's workout. How many times have you said to yourself: "God, if I only knew how much damage was taking place, I would never have done that workout." With "20-20 hindsight", you recognize that over-training can lead to a physical imbalance. Doing more than the body will allow pushes you into the danger zone. The idea of what is enough needs to be re-assessed continually.

The degree of your achievement and satisfaction depends upon how you balance the different parts of your life. The balanced athlete is careful to engender a feeling of equality within the physical, emotional, social, and spiritual elements of life. Focusing on any one area to the exclusion of the others for long periods of time is a sure road to distress, unhappiness, and health problems. Of course you can't have every piece perfectly balanced all the time, but you can strive for some form of equilibrium. How can you lead a more balanced life in order to train well and yet remain healthy and fulfilled each day?

Tools for Creating Balance

Moderation: Know what is enough in each area of your life. Avoid the extremes, especially in athletics, work, eating, and drinking habits. Strive for self-control when tempted to over-indulge in your favorite vices. Balance your work with time for exercise, family, friends, and fun. If you've been giving a good deal of your energy to others, be sure to take time for yourself. Do something healthy that makes you feel good inside. Take care of your body, mind, and spirit each day.

Athletics: To remain motivated, healthy, and balanced as an athlete, try doing more than one sport. You can cross-train, for instance, alternating your running with swimming, biking, or inline skating. You will use various muscle groups and experience a different mindset with each sport. Creating variety in your training is a definite hedge against boredom and burnout.

Eating Habits: Pay attention to your body's need for a proper balance of carbohydrates, protein, and fat. Hydrate with plenty of water after workouts. Create variety and diversity in your meal planning. Become aware of food cravings and avoid binging on unhealthy foods with no nutritional value. Giving yourself a steady balanced diet of fresh, wholesome foods will enhance your sense of well-being and your perspective on life.

Business: Just as there are hard and easy days in athletic training, so there are challenging periods in your job that you need to balance with less demanding intervals. Create more variety in your work so that you engage in an assortment of tasks throughout the day. Develop a more flexible schedule so you allow time for relaxation breaks or exercising at noontime. Choose to work less time during some seasons to allow for more balance in other parts of your life.

The balance in our lives is like the swinging of a pendulum. The more it swings to the right toward peak performance, the more it needs to swing back to the other side for full recovery. There may never be a perfect balance for all parts of our lives, but we can strive to attend to each important element at least sometime during the week. We need to be constantly vigilant about what critical parts of ourselves need more of our attention. With a properly balanced lifestyle we can maintain an inner harmony within ourselves and in our pursuits.

Visualization for Creating Balance:

Close your eyes and begin to breathe deeply. Imagine a circle in front of you where all the pieces of your life can come together. Notice that the circle includes the appropriate amount of time and energy for each important part of your life. See the sections being balanced exactly the way you would like them to be.

Now imagine that you are waking up in the morning, feeling well rested and refreshed. Allow yourself to begin the day, taking a few moments of quiet time to meditate or get centered. See yourself going for a morning workout, feeling energized throughout the day. Imagine what it feels like to make healthy choices – to work hard, play hard, socialize, laugh, exercise, relax, and be spontaneous. Feel the vitality and joy from living a full, balanced life.

Affirmations for Balance:

I am learning to balance the important parts of my life.

I am paying attention to my body's need for a proper balance.

I use a balanced approach to my training.

I know when to push hard and when to back off in my workouts.

I use moderation in my exercise, eating habits, and lifestyle.

I am aware of what is enough in each area of my life.

I am engaging in quality recovery time in order to have balance.

Chapter
23

Attitude Adjustment
in the
Aging Process

Dreams
are not only
for the young

Y ou have probably heard the saying: "The older I get, the faster I used to be." The process of aging does have an effect on athletic performance, and certain physiological changes need to be taken into account when designing your training program. How aging affects you individually depends largely on your attitude and your approach to training. The effects of aging on fitness can vary significantly from one person to the next.

> "Age is a myth." That was Priscilla Welch's comment while celebrating her 43rd birthday two weeks early by winning the overall women's title at the 1987 New York City Marathon. A few months earlier she had set her world masters' record in the marathon by running 2:26:51, a record that still stands today. She said, "Media interviews after my clinics are so boring these days because I'm always asked the same negative question: 'When do you think you're going to slow down?' Obviously this will happen to me sometime. But it's a bad question that has no relevance to me at the moment, because I think there's still a heck of a lot of room for me to improve."

Breaking the Old Rules

Priscilla, along with Bill Rodgers, Jack Foster, Carlos Lopes, Payton Jordan, and many others, appears to have broken the old rules. They seem to have defied the effects of aging that were thought to be "normal." Conventional wisdom held that runners, for instance, were supposed to peak in their twenties and perhaps maintain their fitness level until their mid-thirties. Runners a decade older were not supposed to be running alongside those half their age. However, Jack Foster, from New Zealand, ran the fastest marathon of his life at age 41 in 2:11:19 and set a world masters record. Carlos Lopes, from Portugal, won the 1984 Olympic Marathon at age 37, and at 38 set a world record of 2:07:12. Beyond the sport of running, the same phenomenon is occurring across a wide spectrum of sports.

Although these accounts may seem astonishing, they do not cancel out the natural advantages of youth. They do, however, demonstrate that improvement is still possible after the presumed peak years have passed. This is especially true for people who started exercising later in life. For them the excitement has just begun. Studies have shown that a fit 65-year-old can have the same aerobic fitness as a sedentary 25-year-old. Thus, regardless of one's age, the physical challenges can be similar. Recent research has indicated that seniors who train vigorously can significantly slow down the aging process on the body. We have seen incredible fitness levels with both males and females going into their 80's. Payton Jordan, the legendary track runner, now 83 years old, has been regularly setting new world age-group records during the past three decades for the 100-meters and 200-meters.

> Bill Rodgers, four-time winner of the New York City Marathon and Boston Marathon, is one of the best role models for longevity in sport. At age 53 he is still performing consistently at the top level and owns several masters records. He has run over 700 races, including 58 marathons (28 of them in under 2:16). In his 30 years of competing he has rarely had to take more than three days off from training. He still competes in over 25 races per year.
>
> I asked Bill how he stays motivated to train and compete after all these years. He told me, "It's really just nuts and bolts stuff. I do the same things that have worked for me for years. Before each race I talk to myself. I focus on my specific goals for that particular race. I picture in my mind how I will run the race and how to pace myself. Now that I am older, I've learned to take little mental breaks during each race. I can lay low and recover during parts of the course. It's like shifting gears in a car. I'm always assessing my gauges, asking myself, how am I doing? How much energy do I have left? I try to find a way to make it easier on myself. I tell myself, all you have to do is just do your best."

Re-Framing the Aging Experience

When you hear these inspiring accounts you realize that aging does not need to be the obstacle to fitness it once was. Individuals are emerging from all parts of the world, acting as positive role models while redefining the aging process. They are making a strong statement that you can continue to perform well into your 80's and beyond. You can carry your vitality and fitness for many more years that you ever thought possible. It appears that use or disuse of the body is what determines the rate of physical deterioration. So growing older does not necessarily mean a loss of energy. It does mean that it may be time for an attitude adjustment.

Grete Waitz, nine-time winner of the New York City Marathon, has adapted well to post-competitive life in her 40's. During a run with her in San Francisco, I asked Grete how her attitude has changed from when she was competing at the top level. She said, "Now that I no longer have the pressure to be number one, I am a much happier person. I still run for enjoyment, but I can put more energy into other aspects of my life. Running is far more satisfying now."

How does one adjust to life after the last personal record is set? The long period of improvement will some day run out, and it is critical to develop coping mechanisms to deal with this fact. If you are a triathlete in your late fifties, you may be racing more than a minute or two per mile slower than you did at your best. How can you reframe this experience so that training is still enjoyable? Try looking at it this way: The slowdown in performances with age exists only on the stopwatch. The physical action, the breathing, and the sense of intensity in racing all feel the same. Only the watch shows otherwise. Times change, but feelings do not.

Every person's time will eventually slow down, but the effort and enthusiasm of competing can remain constant throughout an athlete's lifetime. Comparing this year's times with last year's can become a downer. The eventual aging process leads even great masters athletes to slow down year to year. By taking the emphasis off the clock, older athletes can focus on present rather than past achievements.

> Jeff Galloway, 1972 Olympian in the 10,000-meters and regular contributor to *Runner's World Magazine*, is still running strong at age 55. During our interview he described how he has dealt with the aging process: "I have totally given in to time. I no longer care how fast I am running. Now I just want to get my endorphins each day. I've been running for 42 years. The first 22 years were plagued by hundreds of injuries. During the past 20 years I have not been concerned with the stopwatch, and I've had no major problems." I asked Jeff about his attitude toward mental training. He noted, "When you're younger, you can get by on physical talent alone. As you grow older, the mental component becomes far more important."

I asked Dave Scott, six-time winner of the Hawaii Ironman Triathlon, how he remains motivated to train at age 47. "People get lost in the tangle of chasing their past times. What motivates me to keep training is savoring my health. I can go do a workout today with the same conviction I had twenty years ago. My sister, who is my coach, gives us these wicked workouts in the pool. I make it a mental game. I say, OK, can I hold this time throughout each of my intervals? Can I beat my training partner on the last lap? I still derive a lot of enjoyment from my training."

Tips for Attitude Adjustment

Relaxation and recovery: Proper recovery techniques become more critical as we age. After each workout allow extra time to rest and relax. To accelerate the recovery process, do an exercise that includes deep abdominal breathing and mind/muscle relaxation. With your eyes closed, tense and then relax each muscle group throughout the body. Taking time to rest recharges the mind and body. Notice how your energy begins to return and how you can rebound more quickly for your next workout.

Mental stimulation: Read inspiring magazines and books that fuel your mind and body. Study your senior athlete role models, and learn what makes them successful.

Reflection: Take time to consider your journey as an athlete. Look back in your logbook to when you first began exercising, and see how far you've come, both athletically and personally. Remember to appreciate your health, and feel a sense of gratitude for what your body has allowed you to accomplish. Realize that training has both joys and hardships, and that progress comes from a process of learning.

New courses: Instead of being discouraged by training on your usual courses and clocking slower times, find new routes for your workouts, and do different competitions so you can start a clean slate as a master.

Social age-group support: Join a club, preferably one that recognizes weekly participation and honors age-group records at local club meets. Then you can be acknowledged just for participating and for training consistently.

New records: Rather than comparing current performances to your all-time personal records, look toward setting new PR's for each season, for each single age, and each five-year age group.

Change of perspective: Humor can be one of the best ways to create a better attitude in the aging process. Here's an example of how humor can make aging more tolerable and even more fun.

The Stanford Angell Field Ancients is an informal running group that meets regularly to train on Sunday mornings (you may need gray hair to qualify). The group is divided into two sections - the fast group and the slow group. After 50 years of being called the SLOW group, its members were becoming discouraged and wanted to upgrade their name to something a bit more complimentary. After an extended e-mail list discussion about what the name for the new group should be, they finally settled on "the medium group." Then there was a long search for an appropriate acronym for the new name. Here is the announcement of the best titles that emerged:

"Apparently the formerly named S.L.O.W. group (Slowly Losing Our Wheels) has been renamed the M.E.D.I.U.M. group (not to be confused with that other fast group)."

➢ Middle-aged Egomaniacal Dummies Ignoring Unavoidable Mortality
➢ Middle-aged Ex-racers Degenerating Into Unparalleled Mediocrity
➢ Mile-pace Enormously Declines In Unrepentant Masters
➢ Mostly Entertaining Discussion Invigorates Unproductive Miles
➢ Mostly Easy Distance-runs Increase Upcoming Mediocrity
➢ Methodically Eroding "Da trails" In Underwhelming Manner
➢ Many Eccentric Dudes In Undeniable Mediocrity

> Walt Stack, the legendary triathlete, began competing in the Hawaii Ironman in his 70's and continued well into his 80's. Every morning he could be seen in San Francisco's Aquatic Park, swimming in 60-degree water without a wetsuit. He would then hop on his bike, or go for a run across the Golden Gate Bridge. Consistency, rather than speed, was the key to his success and longevity. His trademark slogan was: "Just start slow and then taper off."

© William Dunn

In sum, the equation for healthy aging is as follows: Setting realistic goals, plus longer recovery time, plus attitude adjustment equals continued success and fulfillment. The real barrier to aging and athletic performance appears to be the mind, not the body. How we handle advancing age has a great deal to do with our mindset, our personal beliefs, and our lifestyle. As we train the mind to move beyond its self-imposed limitations, the body will follow.

Mental Training for Energy and Vitality

Prior to each workout take five to ten minutes to visualize what you want to accomplish in your training. See it happening exactly as you wish it to occur. Use positive affirmations to intensify the feelings of self-confidence, power, and inner strength. See yourself moving smoothly, gracefully, and with ease. Reframe any negative thoughts about aging into a positive mindset. Say to yourself: "I can do this. I'll do the best I can with the body that I have today." Make every workout a victory.

Progressive Muscle Relaxation

Harvard physiologist Edmund Jacobson explored the relationship between mental anxiety and muscle tension, and developed a training system for athletes. It's quite simple to learn and utilize. Try doing this exercise following each workout and before going to sleep at night. Begin by doing your 10 deep abdominal breaths. Then go through each part of the body from the toes to the head, tensing and then relaxing each muscle group. You'll find that after you tense a muscle, it will relax more fully and deeply. Imagine that you have a special relaxation tool (e.g., a massager) that you can use to calm down any area of excess tension.

Chapter
24

Putting Performance
in Perspective:
Positive Coaching

*Coaches need to
read their athletes
correctly and
understand them
for who they are*

Sports provide a wonderful training ground for developing one's self-confidence, determination, and inner strength. Individuals can learn leadership skills, competitiveness, cooperativeness, and self-discipline in addition to attaining physical fitness. However, athletics can also become a negative experience for some people if they do not receive the right kind of emotional support from a coach or trainer. Coaches need to be sensitive to the impact that sports experiences can have on their athletes' self-concept and self-esteem.

Coaches need to understand that the lessons gained from athletics are frequently carried over into the rest of a person's life. For instance, the sports setting provides continuous opportunities for comparing oneself with others. People notice how others respond to their performance. The critical reactions of coaches, friends, teammates, opponents, and spectators are often highly visible and are directly felt. Even the more subtle reactions, although unintentionally displayed, are easily picked up by the athlete. The negative reactions over time can have a deep, long-lasting impact, especially on athletes who are emotionally fragile and sensitive to criticism. The process of self-comparison and taking in feedback or criticism from others occurs in any situation where there is human interaction. However, the effects can be softened and viewed more realistically when an understanding coach helps the athlete place the competitive experience in proper perspective.

In fact, the greatest contribution that a coach can provide for an athlete in this regard is character building. One of the best educators of character is the discipline of sports. In addition to encouraging physical fitness, coaches are in a powerful position to foster psychological skills as well. This teaching might involve developing self-assurance, discipline, courage, ability to handle adversity, and leadership skills. Coaches have a unique opportunity to support athletes in their personal growth and development.

However, instead of developing character, many coaches are focused solely on the idea of winning – that is, the professional model. A win-at-all-costs philosophy is required for advancement of coaches in most institutions, and, in fact, for mere survival. Professional coaches do not receive many honors for developing character. Their primary function is to compete successfully for tangible rewards. Their value is based on how much they contribute to winning and profit-making for their teams. In fact, many of the problems in sports occur when coaches incorrectly impose this professional model on what should be an enjoyable and educational experience for amateur athletes.

Common Coaching Mistakes

➤ Overreacting when the athlete makes an error or doesn't perform up to expectations

➤ Demanding too much time or commitment from athletes so that they are overtrained, burned out, or continually injured

➤ Giving an inordinate amount of attention to "the star" and ignoring the value of other team members

➤ Keeping the pressure on so every practice becomes a "life-or-death" situation; requiring that every athlete improve by a certain amount each day

➤ Not respecting that the athlete needs to have balance in his or her life - time for school, work, family, relaxation

➤ Overemphasizing body weight with female athletes, often leading to self-image problems or a serious eating disorder

➤ Mistreating or demeaning the athlete for being lazy, not trying, or not placing high enough

➤ Engaging in inappropriate behavior: harassing officials or opponents or using profanity

➤ Losing perspective of the purpose of sports and being preoccupied with winning, putting the athletes under additional stress

An extreme example of the loss of perspective in athletics comes from the increasing reports of anger and violence occurring during sports events. Take the sportsmanship out of the athletic arena, and what's left is sports rage. In Florida, for instance, an assistant coach of a youth baseball team punched an umpire and broke his jaw. In Massachusetts, a father was beaten to death by another father who was upset over aggressive play between their kids during a hockey practice. In a San Diego gym, a man died after being struck in a basketball game, while another man lost the use of his left eye in the same fight.

Of course, there have always been fights and threats by athletes who think this type of gesturing gives them an edge on the competition. But anecdotal evidence indicates there is an increase in the frequency and severity of explosiveness among both adult and young recreational athletes as well as their coaches and parents. Currently there are no reliable figures to objectively measure the amount of sports violence, since most conflicts are handled between players and are not reported to the authorities. However, one spokesperson for the Wisconsin-based National Association of Sports Officials insists that amateur sports are out of control. Both kids and adults are acting out their aggression much more now than in the past. We frequently see pushing, shoving, and head butting.

Athletes see it going on between the pros on television, and they think it must be acceptable.

Many coaches are no longer spending the time to teach sportsmanship but are more focused on doing whatever it takes to win. Whereas fighting off the field can result in jail time, assaults within the sports arena are often condoned, and players are only benched or suspended temporarily. The sports violence goes far deeper than anger over a disputed play or a bad call by a referee. The individuals who resort to violence are often frustrated about how they are being treated at home, at work, at school, or by their coaches.

What Makes Athletes Angry and Frustrated?

> An atmosphere of continuous negativity during workouts
> Coaches who don't know how to listen or give constructive feedback
> Being singled out as the cause of the team's failure
> Seeing the "star" athlete regularly receive most of the attention and praise
> Not being appreciated for the hard work and extra hours they are contributing
> Not being allowed to rest and recover adequately from workouts
> Feeling the constant pressure to win and be number one

How to Develop Well-Balanced Athletes

Given this information, what can coaches do to make sports a more positive experience for athletes? Coaches need to place training and competing in a healthy perspective and acknowledge that learning comes from both winning and losing. Athletes need to be taught that success is found in striving for the win, not in the outcome itself. The only element that athletes have complete control over is the amount of effort they put forth. They have only a limited amount of influence on the final results of the competition. Outcomes depend upon the fitness of the other athletes, the weather conditions, and countless other factors. Coaches need to impress upon their athletes that they are never losers if they give maximum effort. In this way they are teaching them a valuable lesson that they can use throughout their life's endeavors.

What Coaches Can Do

➤ Emphasize fun, participation, and skill improvement rather than winning and losing: Most people participate in a sport because they enjoy doing the activity for its own sake. The material rewards should be secondary.

➤ Set achievement standards that are within the athlete's capabilities.

➤ Enjoy the successes that occur, and express appreciation for the effort that went into them. Never be punitive or rejecting if the athlete tries but does not succeed. If you want your athlete to avoid fear of failure, do not give him or her a reason to dread failure.

➤ Stress improvement of individual skills rather than comparison to others: Physical growth and skill development occur at different rates for each person. Help every athlete derive pleasure from self-improvement over time, even if the person will never be an Olympian.

➤ Know what level of direction to provide for each athlete: Avoid under- or over-coaching. Some athletes need strong guidance. Others are more self-directed and only need a consultant.

➤ Communicate unconditional acceptance: Provide a basis for positive self-concept by sending a message that each athlete has value whether that individual is a star or a bench warmer.

➤ After a tough loss, listen, support, understand, and praise: Provide an accepting environment for the athlete to fully feel and express the emotion after the event. Respect and accept those feelings. Do not deny or distort what the athlete is feeling. Do not say, "You did great," when he knows he didn't. Instead, point out something positive that was achieved during the competition (e.g., "You maintained good training form throughout"). Focus on the important lessons of life that can be learned (e.g., being mentally strong in the face of adversity, self-discipline, patience, cooperation). Look forward to achieving future goals.

The purpose of an athletic program should be to teach the individual the lessons of training, competition, winning, and losing, and skills for handling any situation that may surface. Coaches should emphasize participation, doing one's best, and letting the activity be its own reward. Every competition will have a winner and loser. The successful program will have a coach who accepts the losing along with the winning and will be able to congratulate each person for his or her efforts. Properly managed, a sports program can be an important training ground for athletes to develop a positive self-image. Athletes can then use the lessons of sport for competing successfully in other areas of life.

© Lloyd Chambers

Interview with Payton Jordan, 1968 U.S. Olympic Coach

Payton Jordan, head coach for the U.S. Olympic team in 1968, provides an excellent example of positive coaching. As one of the world's most respected track and field coaches, his '68 team won more Olympic medals and established more records that any other team in history. He then coached the track and field team at Stanford University for 28 years.

Jordan is also an extraordinary role model for strength and longevity in sport, as he continues to set world masters track records at age 83. Ever since his first race as a 13-year-old at Pasadena Junior High, he has pursued excellence in every aspect of life. In 1939 he was captain of University of Southern California's championship track and field team, and made the cover of *Life Magazine*. In 1941 he ran 9.5 seconds and set a world record for the 100-yard dash on a grass track – a mark that stood for 27 years.

Thirty years later, in 1972, Jordan was the fastest 55-year-old at 100 meters, posting a time of 11.6. He went on to set world masters records at 100 and 200 meters for the next 25 years. At age 81, he ran 100 meters in 14.52 – a time that, adjusted for age, was a hundredth of a second faster than Donovan Bailey's world record mark of 9.84 seconds. Jordan has coached and competed at world-class levels for more than 70 years. His achievements have earned him a collection of Hall of Fame honors.

When I called Payton to arrange for an interview, he said: "I'm not sure if I can meet with you until next week because I'm taking care of my wife (Payton said they have been married for 60 years). You see, my wife and I were out surfing in Santa Barbara last week and a big wave injured her shoulder." The idea of surfing at age 83 gives testimony to how well he has taken care of himself over the years.

JoAnn Dahlkoetter: What elements do you feel are most essential in the psychology of coaching?

Payton Jordan: As a coach, I believe you need to make the activity exciting, interesting, and colorful for athletes. You add to the performance if you do that. You need to make them feel that what they are doing is important. If a person is not inspired, if he doesn't feel there's something special about his sport, he won't perform as well.

This is a part of a motivational tactic that I use in coaching kids. I feel that every kid is important. When you approach a person with an idea, it may sound the same or look the same for each person, but it isn't the same. It's for that person alone. Each athlete needs special attention. The coach can initiate the motivation, but the true action needs to be taken by the individual. The coach starts the fire; then the athlete stokes it.

JD: Through your coaching experience what have you learned about the mind and motivation of athletes?

PJ: I have retired now as a coach, but I don't think you ever really retire, because you are a source of information that can be passed on. People reinvent the wheel all the time. From my standpoint I hear things today that people think are amazingly new, and strangely to me they're not new at all. What puzzles me is when people think they've got the only answer that ever came along. And I think to myself, "Where were you 50 years ago? Were you there to hear that same thing?"

The fundamental concepts of human nature, like the psychology of sports and motivation, really haven't changed a great deal. Even in the early days when people were not so sophisticated, the same things have motivated people in many ways. Maybe they didn't have the same eloquent language to describe them, but people were still driven to be the best that they could be. You had those that rose to the top, those that stayed at the bottom, and those that stayed in the middle. And most of that comes from one's mental attitude. Most people say, it's OK if I'm in the middle. They're satisfied with that – no commitment and no worry. But then there's the guy who wants to be at the top of the pile, and he is willing to make the commitment. The first step to success is commitment.

JD: Did you find yourself striving to be at the top as a young athlete?

PJ: Sure, whenever I signed up for a race I made a commitment to do my best. I also never thought about breaking a record, but I always knew what that record was. I would say, "That I must strive to reach." And I knew that this would take discipline. If I didn't have the discipline, I wouldn't care enough.

Coaches come into the picture here when the discipline is not strong enough in an athlete, and it needs to be reinforced. Then, the second part of discipline is motivation – making people believe and want to reach their goals. In this way the discipline becomes soft and comfortable. But if you scream at people, it won't work. I'm always surprised that screamers think they are getting better action. Talking to people, showing people, leading people, and encouraging people is much more important than the whipping, the fighting, and the threatening. There are times to be very firm, but most of the time you get a lot more done by saying, "Hey, this is going to be fun, isn't it? We are going to get this done." Then the athlete becomes open and starts to dream a little bit. They start to set some goals. You've got to be careful you don't let them go out too far too soon with their goals, where they get shot down or embarrassed. You should make the goals realistic and attainable. Then you stretch them; you stretch those goals all the time, trying to get people to up their target.

JD: Tell me about your experience as U.S. track and field coach for the 1968 Olympics.

PJ: I had an awful lot of great athletes. Many of them would have done well in spite of any coaching. But surprisingly, some of the greatest champions are seeking coaching and hoping someone will care enough to say, "This is what is happening; this is what will help you." We oftentimes think the successful person does not need any support system. Yet the true champions are the most coachable athletes – they are the most open to gaining feedback. A great athlete doesn't need a whole lot of coaching. He or she needs only a little molding, reinforcement, and motivation.

Al Oerter, the four-time Olympic gold medal winner in the discus throw (1956, 1960, 1964, 1968), was one of the greatest athletes of all time. Just think of the dedication, the motivation, and the discipline to go four times. That's 12 years of being at the top of your game every year that the Olympics came around. I coached him in '64 and in '68. He had worked with another coach earlier. When I coached him, in a sense I may have saved him from fading. If he had not been caught a couple of times when he needed help, he may not have gotten the job done. He said to me, "You motivated me when I needed it the most." He told people, "You always knew that coach Jordan would kick you in the butt to get the job done, but he always cared."

JD: So would you say a great coach needs both of those qualities – discipline and concern?

PJ: Yes, you've got to care about the kid; you can't be worried about yourself and your reputation or how great you are. The mistake many coaches sometimes make is that they think they're more valuable than they really are. Coaches can become very important in an athlete's life; they're like a father figure. Kids come to you with all the baggage and hang-ups of their families. The suspicions they have of their mother or their father, the resistance they have to their mother or their father all get dumped right on you. And you get 60-80 of those kids with all their problems. You have to be very careful that you read them right and try to take them for what they are. Then try to bring them to where they need to be for the best personal result.

So it's not wise to yell or demand or ridicule. Because a kid who is sensitive doesn't understand why he is being beaten on when he really wants to perform well, but he doesn't know how. He needs to be shown how, then reinforced and complimented. He has to have someone motivating him to go for more. He needs to learn when to work hard and when to work less. It's just as important to understand when not to work as when to work hard. And you can spend a lot of time working at something that doesn't have anything to do with success. That's where the coaching experience comes into the picture.

JD: Can you give an example of how you would motivate an athlete?

PJ: I do it with a lot of talk and reinforcement. I get them to say something, then I try to put their experience into a positive perspective. Everything needs to be upbeat. If there's a mistake, I don't dwell on the mistake. For instance, I would say, "You're pretty darn good here; now if we can get rid of this over here, we can really get it done." You try to build on their strengths and push the mistake away. If you dwell on the negative, the athlete closes up like a clam, but he really opens up when you compliment and support him. He might have resisted you earlier, but now he begins to listen. The improvement will come more quickly when you have this trusting relationship.

JD: Talk about your association with Jesse Owens. When did you compete against him?

PJ: I ran against him in the 100 yards when I was a kid and he was a young man. That was before we had the 100-meter races. He was four years older than I was. I was a freshman at USC; he was a senior at Ohio State. We ran in races together a couple of times in the LA Coliseum, and we became good friends. I greatly admired him. I knew he was the greatest sprinter in the world at the time. When you go to a track meet as a 17-year-old kid and you're standing next to a 21-year-old man, the best in the world, and you step up to the starting line, you really stop and think. Whenever we raced, I saw his back, and I wasn't the only one. There were a lot of people who never got to see anything but his back.

You just knew when you were around Jesse, the aura of confidence, preparation, and commitment. It exuded from him; you felt it. Some people just walk up to the starting line and you know they are there. They can put the hex on you real quick without saying a word. I know that a good athlete puts out some kind of psychological aura. The radar gets picked up among other athletes. You sense it; you know the guy is gonna do the job. You know that you can't take him lightly. You know you're gonna pay dearly if you do. And that guy is difficult to be around. He just makes you feel: "Well, I guess I'm going to be running for second."

Jesse Owens had that confident quality; it's just the way he carried himself, but never with arrogance. He was gracious; he never looked down at you. Of course he later went on to win four gold medals in the Berlin Olympics. He is looked upon as one of the greatest athletes of all time. He probably has had the strongest influence on track and field of any track athlete in the Olympic games. He raced and won in front of Hitler, when Hitler was trying to make a case for the Aryan supremacy of Nazi Germany. Jesse Owens just flaunted it in front of his face. He ran those gold medals right out of the stadium. It was a great accomplishment. But most of all he was a good person, a great friend, and a guy that I thought a great deal of.

JD: Did you have dreams of being able to run as fast as Jesse Owens?

PJ: When I was racing with Jesse, I wasn't really ready to be in that league with him; I was too young. When you get a little older and stronger with more experience, then you don't back off in races.

But when you're young, you still have doubts. You need more reinforcement, more good training, more nurturing and direction. However, it doesn't come quickly for everybody. Some people have to work a long, long time before they can become a champion.

I remember I was at a clinic one time when Jesse was speaking. There were a lot of young kids in the room. One of the kids said, "Yeah, but Mr. Owens, you're just a natural athlete." Jesse said, "Wait a minute, son, you only become a natural athlete when you've worked very, very hard. Each of you has the opportunity. It's there for you to grab on to. But it's up to you, and it's going to be hard work, but you'll enjoy it."

In fact, the first guy that called me when I became the Olympic coach was Jesse Owens. He said, "Payton, I'm so glad you're going to be our Olympic coach. If there is anything I can do for you, let me know." I said, "Jesse, I would like you to come and speak to our first team meeting at the Olympics." And he did. He said to the group, "Coach Jordan is the right guy because he knows how to relate to people."

You know, we had a lot of turmoil in the Olympics in '68 with the black power movement and all that, and yet we overcame it. We had what they called the greatest Olympic team in history, with more medals and more Olympic and American records than any other team in history. It was a team that was totally dedicated and motivated. They were ready to go in spite of all the distractions. For me it was a fantastic moment to have that kind of group of people to work with.

JD: What advice would you give today's coaches?

PJ: The important thing to remember is that athletes are human. They need a lot of nurturing instead of pressuring or pushing. Coaches need to create opportunities, to clear the path for the athlete to succeed. Athletes need to have the peace of mind that they can trust their coach and know they will not feel threatened. People often fear that they will fail. It is crucial for coaches to teach their athletes that a mistake is not a failure; it's just another step on the road toward success.

JD: You have accomplished so much, and you are a wonderful role model for other coaches and athletes. You appear to be very satisfied with your life.

PJ: Yes, I think of all the kids I have coached over the years. I know 15 of them now have their own children named after me. I have actively competed in track from age 13 to 83. They say that no other track athlete in history has ever had as long a career at world-class level as a sprinter (from 1936-2001). My family has been a wonderful support system. I've had 60 great years of marriage, with two children, four grandchildren, and one great-grandchild. You could say I've had a hell of a good run.

Chapter
25

Sports as a Metaphor
for Life

*Training is the
path to wholeness,
vitality, awareness,
and connection
with life*

Sports involvement at any level can be viewed as a personal journey, a lifetime of discovery and learning. Athletic training is far more than mere physical activity or competition. It offers the opportunity to look deep inside and uncover weaknesses and strengths. The lessons appear on many different levels – mental, physical, and even spiritual - as you open up to them.

Whatever your athletic passion, you can encounter the full range of knowledge and experience that is necessary to be successful in life. The sports setting is like a miniature rehearsal for life's trials, with all of the pleasures and hardships, growth and setbacks, victories and shortcomings that you face in day-to-day living. It provides a path to personal discovery and development. Athletics is the perfect metaphor for understanding how to live your life to the fullest.

Sport teaches us about many aspects of life that would be difficult to learn in any other way. The power and energy of athletics, the feeling of being completely absorbed in an activity, can bring out your absolute best. Competition offers a unique opportunity to challenge yourself, to test your limits, and to perform as you never have before. There are few activities in life that offer the same kind of intensity and accelerated learning as the athletics arena.

The Game of Life

The pursuit of excellence can be both demanding and satisfying. To do well in sports, you are simultaneously learning what it takes to do well in the rest of your life. The principles for distinction in both arenas are the same. The difference between a mediocre athlete and a champion is in the willingness to persevere in the face of adversity. The same is true for a doctor, a computer programmer, a salesperson, or a worker in any other occupation.

The qualities that employers look for in their workers are the same ones that coaches seek in their athletes. Character and integrity come first, followed closely by positive attitude, self-discipline, desire, and commitment. Sales personnel, like athletes, must possess all of these qualities and be highly competitive and mentally tough. The area of sales is nothing more than one-on-one competition, and the sale is rarely made on the first attempt. The best person in sales is the one who refuses to quit until he or she closes the deal. The competitive spirit and tenacity give that individual the edge on the competition.

The Hidden Qualities

Behind the mental toughness and competitiveness, there is another, far deeper level of learning that goes on when you get involved in sports. You may not appreciate this part until you lose a race, or become injured, or sink into a performance slump. For deep fulfillment and personal growth through athletics, you also need to learn about the "softer qualities" of patience, humility, and accepting responsibility for mistakes. You learn to search deep inside to discover your vulnerabilities and your strong points. After you recover from an injury, you expand your appreciation of health and life. Through riding the waves of successes and failures, you learn how to win and how to rebound from defeat. You accept the ups and downs in sport and also in life.

When you train and compete, you will eventually be faced with every conceivable emotional state as you are compelled to respond to many demanding situations. You learn to handle difficult emotions and to express your feelings even when it's uncomfortable to do so. Along with emotional awareness, you may also develop a new sensitivity to your body, so you can tell when it's time to push hard and when you need to rest and recover.

Through these experiences you will develop a firm belief in yourself and faith in your plan. You will know yourself well enough to make wise decisions. You will have an inner direction and a sense of purpose in life. Once these qualities are acquired through sports, they will naturally flow into your professional and personal life. The same belief in your ability as an athlete will allow you to be confident during a job interview or poised in giving a company presentation.

Steve Young, quarterback for the 49ers, retired in June, 2000. In his retirement speech he compared football to the working world: "Most of you get a quarterly or annual review at your job. In my job I get a performance review every 15 seconds. The pressure is always on."

Regarding his feelings about retirement, he said: "Once you leave the sport, it's the relationships you've forged that make all the difference, that allow you to move forward with other aspects of your life. They always told me to go out on top, and that's what I'm doing." Coach Steve Mariucci stood up and said, "Steve, you'll be a far better husband, a better father, a better CEO or sports commentator, or whatever you want to be, now that you are leaving the sport. We'll remember you for all the great plays of course - your assault on the record books. But what stands out in my mind is what happened behind the scenes. I witnessed the kind of person you really are, extremely caring, loving, and generous."

Lessons of Life from Sports

There are many parallels between athletics and your day-to-day living. Let's discuss how you can incorporate the lessons of sports into your personal and professional life.

Positive Vision

Find your passion and follow your path. In sports and life you need to find out what you love doing and carry it out with your heart and soul. Discover an activity that is meaningful for you and beneficial to others. Follow your intuition, and choose the path that serves you best. Then move forward on your course with passion and commitment. Stay true to your dreams regardless of what others say. When you enjoy what you are doing and know you are pursuing worthwhile goals, anything is possible.

> Michael Johnson was often asked about his unorthodox running form. Here is how he responded:
>
> "Some people think it looks different, some people think it's strange. What do I call it? How about beautiful! I think the best description is, effective. My style is more smooth, more effortless than most of the people I'm running with. Some coaches were leery at first. They'd think, Yeah, he'll be really good when I change his style."
>
> But the irony is that this funny running style of his is actually a quick-cadenced, biomechanical marvel – a huge factor behind his mind-boggling speed.
>
> Michael noted: "A lot of commentators would say, 'God, if he changed his running style, if he ran like everybody else, just imagine what he could do.' Yeah, I say, if I ran like the other guys, I'd be right back there with everybody else."

What is your true passion in sports? What turns you on and energizes you in life? Are you allowing enough time for these things?

The best performers in athletics, education, the arts, and business do what they love and love what they do. They pursue their goals for the pure joy of engaging in that activity. They invest so much of themselves in the activity because they see their goals as rewarding and worthwhile. Thus, they can continue to create with excitement and vision.

Playfulness and Fun

You can work extremely hard toward your future goals both in sports and in life, but you don't need to sacrifice the rest of your life to arrive there. It is possible to balance working hard and playing hard while having a fulfilling life in the here and now. You can achieve your dreams and have fun in the process.

No matter how intense things become in your life, always leave time for play. Nothing should get in the way of laughter and fun; they allow you to lighten up and keep life in perspective. Play can enrich your life as much as any other goal or achievement. It cleanses your spirit, recharges your batteries, and allows you to return to work with renewed enthusiasm. Keep playfulness at the center of your life. Create an opportunity to laugh or play at least once per day.

> I had a client ask me about an article he was reading in a magazine. He said: "Dave Scott was talking about lactate threshold. But later he was also talking about nutrition and including a lot of milk in your diet." The client then asked me, "So what is this lactate threshold anyway? Does it have something to do with milk?" I laughed and told him, "Oh, you've reached your lactate threshold when you've consumed the most milk you can possibly drink."

Do you view your workouts as a time for work or play? Perhaps there should be time for both. You can play both in sports and in life. Remember when you first discovered your sport? Can you recapture that feeling of spontaneity and curiosity, the feeling of total absorption in your activity, of being in the moment? You can bring back a simple focus, having a mind that is free from anxiety and distractions, with no concern about the judgments of others. You can become totally connected to what you are involved in at each moment, whether it is doing an interval workout or writing a proposal for your supervisor at work. You can enjoy a fresh outlook each day and look forward to continuous learning in athletics and in life. Never forget the power of play.

Appreciation For Life

Recognize the value of your journey in sports and in life, and realize all that you have gained. As you look back on the road you have traveled, you can take a broader view and acknowledge the multitude of goals you have achieved along the way. Remember all the friends you have met and the opportunities that have come your way. Realize how much your body has allowed you to accomplish, and treasure the fun and satisfaction you've experienced. You will identify a whole host of benefits you have received without your conscious awareness.

Cathy Freeman, 2000 Olympic gold medalist in the 400-meters, related: "I remember as a child this sense of being inferior, that we had no right to be in a white restaurant, or a white store. There's always a sense of loss, with all that was taken away from us. We were taken away from our homes and put into orphanages and camps. It makes me very sad, but also very determined. I carried both Aboriginal and Australian flags at the last World Championships. Now I am proud of my origins. The effect I have on children is a by-product of what I do best. I am very honored. I feel proud."

Cathy Freeman's victory in Sydney was one of the most stirring moments in Olympic history. She is the definition of grace under pressure. Her winning of the 400-meters is a representation of the way things are supposed to be.

Practice the discipline of gratitude on a daily basis. Enjoy and savor every moment of the day. Take time to appreciate each experience in life, and connect with the precious friends and family around you. Remind yourself to look for the simple joys before beginning each day and before starting each new activity. Find meaning and value in everything you do. Let those special moments, people, and pleasures enrich your body, mind, and spirit. Remember where you came from, and be grateful for your accomplishments. Be thankful that you have another day to live.

In Aug. 2000, just 32 days before the Sydney Olympics, Lance Armstrong was in a serious bike accident with an oncoming car in France. His bike was broken into 3 pieces, and his helmet was completely shattered. In an interview just before the Olympics, Lance noted: "If you saw the bike, you would be surprised that I am alive right now." Two X-rays and an MRI revealed his cracked vertebrae. On Sept 16th, just 18 days after the accident, he won a grueling bike race in France. Can you imagine anyone else coming back that soon? Lance went on to win the bronze medal in the 2000 Olympics. He noted: "I came here to win, but I got the bronze medal. I'm happy about that. Considering all that has happened, I really can't complain."

Your Performing Edge

Finally, the journey of athletics teaches you to take risks, to challenge yourself, to stretch your limits. You can learn to think, train, and feel like a champion, and keep the Olympic spirit with you every day. Follow your dreams, and pursue what is most important to you with vision and passion.

When you consider all those who have lived before us and all those who will come after, our lifetime is relatively short. So live your life to the fullest with vitality and intensity. Be present each step of the way. Train for the pure enjoyment of moving your body. When you are running, run; when you are working, work; when you are outside, open up your senses to your environment and let it heal you. Capture the energy of the moment.

When you do an activity purely to enjoy the process, you become open to the most fulfilling moments in sports and in life. There is no external reward at stake. You require no praise or honor for your accomplishment. There is no need for others to see or even know what you are doing. The value is internal and exists in the doing. You do it for its own reward.

The Same Principles Apply

Athletics challenges the body, mind, and spirit. Competition develops awareness, self-confidence, cooperation, and sensitivity to yourself and others. The same traits apply to academics and the work environment. Learning and working require the same energy and commitment as competitive sports, and they yield the same kinds of benefits. Sports and learning go well together to help people discover and realize their true potential in life. If athletics can give you an inner desire, courage, and determination, and you can combine that with a firm belief in yourself, you'll be hard to beat in the game of life.

Our way of life is perfectly expressed through our physical training. All of the strengths that make up our humanity – the passion, the competition, the pressures, and the willingness to overcome adversity – are found in the spirit of sport.

As you grow both athletically and personally, you'll open up to the value in yourself. When you keep the right perspective in your training, regardless of the final outcome, you are bound to emerge from the sports experience a better person. You'll discover that your voyage has no final destination. The purpose of traveling is for continual growth and renewal as you keep enhancing the definition of what is possible.

About the Author

JoAnn Dahlkoetter, Ph.D., best-selling author of *Your Performing Edge,* is an internationally recognized performance consultant and world-class athlete. She is a licensed psychologist and medical staff member at Stanford University Medical Center. She is past winner of the San Francisco Marathon in 2:43:20, placed 2nd in the Hawaii Ironman Triathlon, and was rated the No. 1 triathlete in the U.S. by *Triathlete Magazine.* Dr. Dahlkoetter has appeared on ABC's *Wide World of Sports* and NBC's *Sports World.* Her work has been published in the *Journal of Consulting and Clinical Psychology, Runner's World,* and *Fitness Runner Magazine*, and she has been featured in *Newsweek* and *Sports Illustrated.* She is currently a regular contributor to several national magazines, including *Triathlete Magazine* and *Running Times.*

Dr. Dahlkoetter is a Diplomate in the field of Sports Psychology. In her 20 years of clinical practice she has worked with numerous Olympic and professional athletes, top business executives, performing artists, and those in high stress careers. She has been on the faculty at the University of California at Berkeley, and she frequently conducts workshops for corporations, universities, and sports clinics worldwide. She currently maintains a full-time private practice and continues to train and race in the San Francisco Bay Area. Her work with champion athletes and top-level business executives gives her special insight into using the mind-body connection to achieve the best in personal performance. Her work includes:

- Keynotes for corporations, universities, and sports clinics
- Performance assessments and evaluations
- Teleseminars and distance learning
- Workshops and expo presentations
- Personal lifestyle and executive coaching
- Sport psychology sessions
- Consulting for individuals and corporations
- Writing feature articles and syndicated columns

For more information, e-mail: info@sports-psych.com
www.YourPerformingEdge.com

Resources Guide

Magazines
Running Times, (800) 816-4735, www.RunningTimes.com
Triathlete Magazine, (800) 441-1666, www.Triathletemag.com
Runner's World, (800) 666-2828, www.RunnersWorld.com
Runner-Triathlete News, (281) 759-0555, www.RunnerTriathleteNews.com
Peak Running Performance, (888) PEAKRUN, www.peakrun.com
Northwest Runner, (800) 825-5629, www.nwrunner.com

Websites
www.YourPerformingEdge.com – Personal Coaching, Performance Articles
www.RunningAndRacing.com -Marty Liquori's ESPN TV program
www.USATriathlon.org - Triathlons, Matt Haugen, US Tri Team Coach
www.TheSchedule.com – Schedule of Running and Triathlon Races
www.DaveScottInc.com – Dave Scott's Athletic Training
www.AvonRunning.com – Women's running programs
www.BillRodgers.com – Running Store
www.LanceArmstrong.com - Cycling
www.Ironteam.org - Leukemia Society Ironman Training
www.ZapFitness.com - Sports Training Camps
www.Telford-Design.com – Mountain Unicycling
www.TeamInTraining.org – Leukemia Society Training
www.VenuSports.com – Women's Sports
www.MarkAllenOnline.com – Mark Allen's Fitness Training
www.DanObrien.com – Training Website
www.Jeff Galloway.com – Training for Runners
www.Ironwomantriathlon.com - Women First Triathlon Consulting, Lisa Lynam

Books
It's Not About the Bike, Lance Armstrong, Putnam Press
20 Years of Cycling, Graham Watson, Velo News Press
Lifetime Running Plan, Bill Rodgers, Harper-Collins Press
Joan Samuelson's Running for Women, Joan Benoit Samuelson, Rodale Press
Alberto Salazar's Guide to Running, Alberto Salazar, McGraw-Hill
Workouts for Working People, Mark Allen and Julie Moss, Random House
Dan O'Brien's Guide to Gold Medal Performance, Hyperion Press
The New Marathon, Jeff Galloway, Phidippides Press
Dave Scott's Triathlon Training Book, Dave Scott, Simon & Schuster
Running & Walking for Women over Forty, Katherine Switzer, St. Martins Press
Parachuting: The Skydiver's Handbook, Dan Poynter and Mike Turoff, ParaPublishing
Sports Endurance, Scott Tinley, Rodale Press
Marathon Training, Joe Henderson, Human Kinetics
Running Past 50, Rich Benyo, Human Kinetics

Photo Descriptions

Your Performing Edge
Top Ten Training Tips
JoAnn Dahlkoetter, Ph.D.

Mindfulness: Practice being in the present moment. Remind yourself to stay in the here and now. Let past and future events fade into the background.

Conscious Breathing: If you change the way you breathe, you can change the way you feel. Breathing abdominally helps you relax and expand your consciousness. Relaxation does for the mind what stretching does for the body.

Power Imagery: Visualization is not something you do only in the quiet of your home. Use your mental images throughout the workout to create feelings of speed and power. (e.g., When you come to an unexpected hill visualize a magnet pulling you effortlessly to the top).

Positive Attitude: Use everything in the workout to your advantage. For example, if another athlete passes you, tuck in behind and go with his or her energy for as long as possible. You may catch a "second wind" and be carried on to a new personal record.

Short-term goals: Focus on your immediate target. Break your training down into small, manageable pieces and begin to focus only on the first portion, not the entire workout (e.g., Say to yourself: "I'm just relaxing and getting my rhythm during the first mile").

Association: Pay close attention to your tension level and training form. Do a body scan while working out and relax your tight muscles frequently. Ask yourself: "Are my shoulders and neck relaxed; how does this pace feel; how much energy is left in my legs?"

Pain Management: If you have "good pain" that is not seriously damaging your body, just shift attention to your breathing or cadence of movement, and let the discomfort fade into the background. You can also use the pain as feedback. Register it not as pain but as effort level. Say: "Now I know exactly how hard I'm working. My body is doing what it should be doing."

Focused Attention: Be aware of distractions. Breathe out unwanted thoughts with your next exhale and re-focus your attention instantly on what is important.

Affirmations: Make positive self-statements continually. Negative thinking is quite common; everyone has an inner critic. Become aware of these thoughts early on. Don't fight with them; simply acknowledge their presence and then substitute a positive affirmation. (e.g., When you're thinking: "This hurts too much," say to yourself: "This feeling is connected with going faster and doing my best").

Enjoyment: Celebrate your fitness and strength. When the competition arrives, let your body do what you've trained it to do. Remember that your goals are realistic. All you need to do is perform up to your capabilities.

For more training tips visit:
www.YourPerformingEdge.com

Personal Coaching

Realize Your Potential
Telephone or In-Office Sessions
JoAnn Dahlkoetter, Ph.D.

Discover Your Performing Edge
Create the right environment for a major
breakthrough in your performance in sports,
health, business, and life. Develop a mindset
that is calm, visionary, and open to the full
range of possibility. This personalized coaching program will empower you to
emerge as a stronger, more successful and fulfilled individual regardless of
your age or ability level.

You will benefit from:
- ➢ A weekly personalized learning experience with JoAnn Dahlkoetter, Ph.D.
- ➢ Regularly scheduled support, coaching, and realistic feedback
- ➢ Motivational e-mail messages and articles tailored to your needs
- ➢ A wealth of ideas and discussion about your specific concerns
- ➢ Ready-to-use techniques and exercises to accelerate your progress
- ➢ A personal coach to help you move forward with your vision and goals

Using this complete formula for success, you will:
- ➢ Achieve the optimal state of mind to perform your best under any conditions
- ➢ Gain new motivation and confidence to break through mental barriers
- ➢ Unleash the power of your mind, body, and spirit to realize your full potential
- ➢ Create a healthy, balanced lifestyle, athletically, professionally, and personally
- ➢ Deal with fear of success and fear of failure
- ➢ Handle stress, anxiety, and health concerns
- ➢ Address weight, eating habits, and body image issues
- ➢ Find new ways to catch your dreams and launch them into reality

Personal coaching is convenient and affordable: You call in on your
telephone from your home or office at a regularly scheduled time. Sessions are
easy to arrange, regardless of your location. Visit the website below for more
information, and send an email or call to set up a phone appointment time.

Book And Tape Order Form

Online Orders: **www.YourPerformingEdge.com**
Postal Orders: Pulgas Ridge Press, Box 730, San Carlos, CA 94070-0730
E-mail: info@sports-psych.com
Telephone Orders: (650) 654-5500

Your Performing Edge: The Complete Mind-Body Guide for Excellence in Sports, Health and Life, **by JoAnn Dahlkoetter, Ph.D.**
This book presents a comprehensive step-by-step program to help you focus your energies, overcome obstacles to excellence, and achieve greater personal and professional fulfillment in all areas of life.

Optimal Performance Visualization Tape **by JoAnn Dahlkoetter, Ph.D.**
This 60-minute tape contains powerful mental training exercises for people at all levels in any sport. These exercises can produce significant improvements in your performance while speeding up your recovery from stress, fatigue, and injuries.
Side One: Optimal Performance Visualization (Thirty minutes)
Side Two: Accelerated Healing and Renewal from Training (Thirty minutes)

Please send me _____ copies of the book: *Your Performing Edge*.
Please send me _____ copies of *Optimal Performance Visualization Tape*.
Please send me _____ your FREE E-mail Newsletter with training tips
PLEASE PRINT CLEARLY:
Name: _____
Address: _____
City: _____ State: _____ Zip: _____
Telephone: _____ E-mail: _____

Please send more information on:
_____ Personal Lifestyle Coaching (Telephone or In-Office Sessions Available)
_____ Sports Psychology Coaching (Telephone or In-Office Sessions Available)
_____ Speaking Engagements/Teleseminars

Sales Tax: California residents add 8%
Shipping: US - $4.95 for the first product, $2.00 for each additional product
International: $11.00 US for the first product, $5.00 for each additional product

Payment: _____ Check_____ Cash
Make checks payable to: **Pulgas Ridge Press**
Books _____ x $16.95
Tapes _____ x $ 14.95 (When you buy the book, the tape is only $11.95)
Tax _____
Shipping_____   **Total** _____

Your Performing Edge
Free Newsletter and Website
The Complete Online Resource

Now that you've read the book, you're ready to move forward. Stay in tune with the latest mind-body techniques for excellence in sports, health, business, and life. Check out our website and newsletter to find fresh, creative solutions to your personal challenges.

Mind-Body Tools
  ➢ Valuable training tips and articles every month
  ➢ Self-assessment tools to determine your needs and goals
  ➢ Personal interviews with the world's greatest athletes
  ➢ Success strategies you can put to use right away
  ➢ A continuous resource of mental skills for sports, health, and life

Free E-mail Newsletter
  Receive regular success tips, inspirational stories, quotes from champion athletes, and motivational articles from leading experts in peak performance, and personal development.
  This monthly e-mail newsletter is packed with advice for achievement and fulfillment in sports and in every aspect of life. To subscribe, just send an e-mail to: newsletter@sports-psych.com. Write "subscribe" in the subject line. Your e-mail address will never be provided to anyone at any time.

  ➢ Build your confidence and self-image
  ➢ Develop mental toughness
  ➢ Focus your energies and sharpen concentration
  ➢ Learn to listen to the wisdom of the body
  ➢ Use creative imagery to realize your goals
  ➢ Acquire a positive perspective
  ➢ Heal mental and physical wounds
  ➢ Learn to use the language for success
  ➢ Create balance in your life

> **Visit: www.YourPerformingEdge.com**
> **E-mail: newsletter@sports-psych.com**

Book And Tape Order Form

Online Orders: **www.YourPerformingEdge.com**
Postal Orders: Pulgas Ridge Press, Box 730, San Carlos, CA 94070-0730
E-mail: info@sports-psych.com
Telephone Orders: (650) 654-5500

Your Performing Edge: The Complete Mind-Body Guide for Excellence in Sports, Health and Life, **by JoAnn Dahlkoetter, Ph.D.**
This book presents a comprehensive step-by-step program to help you focus your energies, overcome obstacles to excellence, and achieve greater personal and professional fulfillment in all areas of life.

Optimal Performance Visualization Tape **by JoAnn Dahlkoetter, Ph.D.**
This 60-minute tape contains powerful mental training exercises for people at all levels in any sport. These exercises can produce significant improvements in your performance while speeding up your recovery from stress, fatigue, and injuries.
Side One: Optimal Performance Visualization (Thirty minutes)
Side Two: Accelerated Healing and Renewal from Training (Thirty minutes)

Please send me _____ copies of the book: *Your Performing Edge*.
Please send me _____ copies of *Optimal Performance Visualization Tape*.
Please send me _____ your FREE E-mail Newsletter with training tips
PLEASE PRINT CLEARLY:
Name: _____
Address: _____
City: _____ State: _____ Zip: _____
Telephone: _____ E-mail: _____

Please send more information on:
_____ Personal Lifestyle Coaching (Telephone or In-Office Sessions Available)
_____ Sports Psychology Coaching (Telephone or In-Office Sessions Available)
_____ Speaking Engagements/Teleseminars

Sales Tax: California residents add 8%
Shipping: US - $4.95 for the first product, $2.00 for each additional product
International: $11.00 US for the first product, $5.00 for each additional product

Payment: _____ Check_____ Cash
Make checks payable to: **Pulgas Ridge Press**
Books _____ x $16.95
Tapes _____ x $ 14.95 (When you buy the book, the tape is only $11.95)
Tax   _____
Shipping_____   **Total**   _____